Teaching Playwriting
The Essential Handbook

A step-by-step guide to fostering creativity in your classroom.

Sophia Chapadjiev

A Beat by Beat Book
www.bbbpress.com

Published by Beat by Beat Press
www.bbbpress.com
Copyright © 2017 Sophia Chapadjiev

All rights reserved. No part of this book may be reproduced or transmitted in any form or by any means, electronic or mechanical, including photocopying, recording or any other storage and retrieval system, without the written permission of the author or publisher.

ISBN-10: 0692848509
ISBN-13: 978-0692848500

As teachers, one of the biggest gifts we can give our students is the encouragement to express themselves creatively.

Teaching Playwriting

The Introduction 1
How to Use This Book 2
At a Glance: Choosing the Right Track for Your Class 3

The Basics

1. What Is a Play? And Where Do Stories Come From? 5
2. Dialogue and Conflict 11
3. Plot Sequencing 19
4. Creating Character I – from a Photo 25
5. Creating Character II – from Random Props 31
6. Creating Character III – from Improvisation 36
7. The Monologue 40

The Practicum

8. Track Work 46
9. Track I: Individual Playwright Plays 47
10. Track II: Small Group Plays 52
11. Track III: Entire Class Plays 58
12. Review, Revision, Rubric 67

The Bonuses

13. The Playwright's Checklist 70
14. Miscellaneous Advice 72
15. Additional Character Activities 74
16. Additional Dialogue Activities 78
17. Performance Crash Course 81
18. Opportunities for Young Playwrights 89
19. Vocabulary 90
20. Worksheet Index 92

The Worksheets

Comparing Different Types of Text .... A
Play Excerpt I: *The Foxwoods Dilemma* .... B
Plot Diagram C
The Eight W's of Character Development .... D
House A .... E
House B .... F
Play Framework .... G
Script Formatting .... H
Play Excerpt II: *The Ivy League* I

The Introduction

How exciting! You have decided to embark on a creative journey with your students. In this day and age, where test prep is paramount, and computer games and social media are how we seem to spend more and more of our free time, things like play-making, role-playing and good old imagination are being relegated to vintage games of yesteryear. And yet, you – by deciding to write plays with your students – are putting creativity back in the spotlight.

Happily, playwriting does all sorts of good things in terms of connecting to creative writing curriculum standards. So, take faith in knowing that in addition to stimulating imaginations, you are also checking off essential educational boxes. By the end of this book, not only will your students have written a play – either on their own or with some of their peers – but they will also have engaged in developing compelling characters, written believable dialogue, experimented with story arc and narrative, and collaborated with their peers. But first things first, yes?

When I was little and I played the piano, a new piece of sheet music would be daunting to contemplate. How could I, as a twelve-year-old – with such limited skills and child-like finger-span – play a minuet or a mazurka written by the likes of Bach or Chopin? My mother would sit me at the piano, set the timer and I would begin. First with the left hand. Then with the right. Taking each measure separately and slowly. Mistakes were made, my goodness were they made. But eventually, after many moons, each hand could master their part. Once they knew what to do individually, the next goal was to put them together. But they are doing such different things! Like patting one's head and rubbing one's belly at the same time, it seemed an impossible task. And then one day – as if by osmosis – music, as Bach and Chopin intended it, happened. Well, maybe not exactly as they'd intended it, but both my mother and I were impressed.

It's like the day you suddenly can ride a bike without training wheels. Weeks of falling over and then one moment, bam, you're balanced for life. None of this would happen without the falling or the practicing. None of it would happen without knowing the basics first.

And that's what this book begins to address. Think of it as a primer for playwriting. The first half focuses on craft like character and dialogue and conflict and plot. And the second half basically says, go on then, put them together, you creative being, you, and see what art you can make.

I wish you and your students fun on this journey. Now go on, you creative beings, you, and go see what art you can make.

Sincerely,

Sophia

How to Use This Book

I'd recommend that all classes – regardless of playwriting experience – begin with **The Basics**. Before students dive into writing plays, it's useful for them to know what plays are, how they differentiate from other literary forms, and where ideas can come from. From there, dialogue, conflict and plot are introduced and explored. And then it is onto character work. In this book, creating character is approached in three different sessions. One of these approaches to character will suffice and yet, if you have time, feel free to try more than one method to give students options into generating character. The Basics section then rounds out with monologue work.

Before you are completely through The Basics, decide which track you want your class to follow in **The Practicum** – that way you can already start tailoring your lessons to your eventual track. An overview of the three different tracks can be found on page 3, but in a nutshell: Track I is for plays written by individuals; Track II is geared towards plays written by small groups; and Track III focuses on a play written by an entire class. If you or your students are new to playwriting, consider choosing Track II or III.

Most sessions commence with a review or a "Do Now" before moving on to activities, and then closing with reflection and follow-up. Within the chapters, you will also find shaded boxes offering teaching advice, side-coaching suggestions, text samples and vocabulary words.

I'd recommend, if possible, that students have a dedicated playwriting folder or notebook where new ideas can be jotted and where vocabulary notes, character sketches and completed writing exercises can be stored and accessed for future reference. You never know when a simple writing activity can germinate into a full-fledged new play idea. Be sure to also check out **The Bonuses** for additional material and follow-up activities and **The Worksheets** section for handouts referred to throughout the book.

I think ten sessions would be a good approximation for the duration of this project – and yet it can certainly be done in less or more time depending upon the needs of your class and the time you have to dedicate to the unit. In terms of target age group, I have used these methods with students ranging from 10 to 18 years of age and yet most of the activities can be adapted for younger – and even older students.

Lastly a note on play length… I recommend quality over quantity any day and so I would stay away from attempting full-length plays, focusing instead on the short play format. To that extent, I would suggest plays be approximately 10-15 pages for individuals and small groups and then 20-25 pages for a class written play.

At a Glance: Choosing the Right Track for Your Class

Track I Play by INDIVIDUAL	Track II Play by SMALL GROUP	Track III Play by ENTIRE CLASS
The individual student is responsible for creating original character and storyline, then writes play entirely on own.	3 to 5 students write a play as a group. They collaborate on creating characters as well as a plot. Each individual is then responsible for the writing of one scene (or moment) of the play.	The entire class will work on a single play. Students will be responsible for creating characters as a group and then writing scenes also in groups.
Recommended for setting where homework is allowed and students are eager to write and are self-motivated. Ideal for drama groups and creative writing classes.	Recommended for a language arts course setting where the bulk of the work is done in class. Good for slightly older students.	Recommended for classes with a particular theme or writing focus in mind. Best suited for younger students.
Advantages: - Ownership of an entire idea from beginning to end - Able to submit to young playwright festivals which don't often take group works Disadvantages - Teacher has a large number of plays to read, grade, and/or comment on - More difficult to have all plays shared aloud	Advantages: - Able to rely on team for inspiration and collaboration - Output of only 4-5 plays has more of a likelihood that all can be shared aloud Disadvantages - Slight chance of play choppiness unless someone is overseeing transitions to make it seamless - Students perhaps limited in only writing one scene	Advantages: - Teacher able to oversee play's theme and shape - 20-30 minds sometimes better than a single one - Can enhance a subject already being studied Disadvantages - Not every student will get a chance to perform - Individual writing voice does not get featured - Some may not contribute as much as others

1   What Is a Play? And Where Do Stories Come From?

While young people have instant access to technological forms of entertainment and culture – television, internet, movies – for some of them, live theater is a bit of a mystery. They also, generally speaking, have more experience reading books than reading plays. Since students are more used to screens and books than stages and plays, it is important to establish:

- What a play is
- How a play is different from a movie
- How it is different from other creative writing forms

Explore: Plays versus Movies

First ask, "Who has ever seen a play before?" to gauge the room's exposure to theater. If hands are raised ask, "What plays have you seen?" Sometimes, instead of a play, a musical like *Oklahoma* or *The Nutcracker* ballet are mentioned. Take the opportunity to discuss the differences between these live mediums, if it comes up.

On the board, write two headings: "Plays" and "Movies". Brainstorm with students a list of what makes these two topics different. When you feel you've covered the differences (and similarities) thoroughly, write the definition of a play on the board.

Vocabulary   Play – A literary piece meant to be performed live by actors (usually on a stage).

Have students pair up and give them a few minutes to come up with a list of ideas for the following two questions:

1. What are some things that can happen in a play that, typically, wouldn't happen in a movie?

2. What are some things that can happen in a movie that, typically, wouldn't happen in a play?

Discuss responses as a group. While movies utilize technology (special effects, multiple camera shots, editing), plays are *live* and *immediate*. There are no second chances or retakes, which means anything can happen in a play and every performance is unique and potentially unpredictable. An audience's energy can also affect a play and its actors, whereas a movie and its actors' performances do not alter once the film is complete.

Activity: Comparing Written Texts

As a class, brainstorm a list of different forms of creative writing.

> **Examples**: novels, short stories, comic books, poems, plays, songs, graphic novels, fairy tales, myths, memoirs

Then, read the following three texts aloud or ask for volunteers to read them in front of the class. If you'd like to make copies to have students read out loud in pairs, a one-page worksheet is in the back of the book (worksheet A).

After the texts have been read aloud, in pairs, have students list the similarities and differences between the three texts. Then, discuss as a class.

Text 1 – Short Story

Ali, a shy, but proud girl, is sitting by herself in a busy café pretending to read a book. She has a cup of tea and a half eaten tuna sandwich in front of her. Every once in awhile she looks at the empty seat next to her and quietly mumbles something towards it. Just as she is about to randomly turn the page of her book, Jay walks by. "Is this seat taken?" he asks. Ali doesn't want to be rude, but she can't allow Jay to sit there because as far as she's concerned, the seat may look empty, but it is actually taken… by her guardian angel.

Text 2 – Poem

> A girl in a café
> Pretends to read a book
> All the while mumbling
> But no one gives a look
>
> A boy who's bought his lunch
> Spies an empty chair
> And asks the girl who's reading,
> "Mind if I sit there?"
>
> The girl cannot allow
> The boy to sit and eat
> 'Cause her invisible guardian angel
> Is sitting in that seat

Text 3 – Play

In a busy café.

JAY: Excuse me. Is this seat taken?

ALI: Um… well… *(She closes the book.)* It kind of is.

JAY: Oh, well, do you mind if I sit here till your friend arrives?

ALI: What makes you think I'm waiting for somebody?

JAY: Um. Okay. *(He goes to pull the seat back.)* I'm just going to sit –

ALI: No, don't!

JAY: Why not?

ALI: Just – just please don't.

JAY: Why?

ALI: It's – it's going to sound stupid.

JAY: Lady, there's nowhere else to sit.

ALI: *(Pausing slightly before speaking.)* My guardian angel is sitting there.

JAY: *(Smiling.)* Your guardian angel.

ALI: I knew you wouldn't believe me.

JAY: Look if you didn't want me to sit there, you could have just said so.

ALI: I *don't* want you to sit there!

Explore: Write or Wright?

Now that you've established the differences between plays and movies, as well as compared plays to two other types of creative writing, it's helpful to understand *who* does *what*. Ask your students:

- What do you call a person who writes a book?   **An author.**
- What do you call a person who writes a poem?   **A poet.**
- What do you call a person who writes a movie?   **A screenwriter.**
- What do you call a person who writes a play?   ***A playwright.***

Vocabulary   Playwright – The person who writes the play.

Point out that the noun is spelled "-wright" as opposed to "-write". Originally, a "wright" was known as a builder or creator of something. And so a playwright is a builder and creator of plays.

Explore: What Makes a Good Story?

Ask students to name a few of their favorite plays, books or movies. Why is it their favorite? What do they like best about it? Challenge them to be both specific and succinct, and to also pick a defining moment in the story.

Examples:
- When Dorothy gets swept up by the tornado
  (*Wizard of Oz*)
- When a pair of sneakers fall out of the sky and hit Stanley Yelnats in the head on his way home from school
  (*Holes*)
- When Scrooge is visited by Jacob's ghost
  (*A Christmas Carol*)
- When Elsa uses her powers to build an ice castle
  (*Frozen*)

Make three columns on the board, categorizing their examples under:

Character	Event	Setting
(Dorothy)	(tornado)	(Kansas)

Another way of looking at it would be:

Who	What	Where

Point out that the stories they like usually have interesting things happening to compelling characters. As a group, brainstorm some new characters, events and settings that could be part of a formula to a new story. For example:

Character: dentist, archeologist, librarian, pilot, middle schooler, dancer

Event: saving a cat, proposing to somebody, buying a gift, attending a protest, leaving one's homeland, breaking a promise

Setting: a factory, the mall, an office, at home, the airport, at school

Activity: Where Do Stories Come From?

Stand in front of the class and begin to tell a story. Start the story off simply, then get more dramatic. At a pivotal moment in the story, ideally a few minutes in, call on a student to take over the storytelling. Let the student continue for a bit and then call on another student to take over. Continue to call on different students until a good number (if not all) have had a chance to contribute. If the story ever falters, grab the reins again until it is back on track with another soon-to-be pivotal moment to hand over to another student. When you feel the story is ready to come to a close, end it.

As a group, take a moment to review some of the characters, events and settings of the story.

Get students' reactions to this activity. Was it fun / easy / hard? What was their favorite part of the story? Then ask them where their ideas for the story came from? Elicit a few different responses till you are able to sum it up with one word – *Everywhere*.

> ***First Sentence Prompt for a Possible Story:***
>
> *There was an old man named Frederick Almstead the Third who lived on a quiet street in a quiet town not too far from a bird sanctuary…*

Activity: *The Foxwoods Dilemma*

Tell your students that they are going to read the opening scene from a play called *The Foxwoods Dilemma* by Micah Greenleaf. Share with them that Micah was in 8th grade when he wrote and submitted *The Foxwoods Dilemma* to the Eugene O'Neill Theater Center's Young Playwrights Festival. It was the first play he ever wrote. Now, Micah is a junior in college majoring in playwriting and screenwriting. From 8th grade beginnings just might come the initial spark that lights up a bright theatrical career.

Hand out copies of the one-page text found in the back of the book (worksheet B). In groups of three, have students read the play out loud with one another. After they are all done, review any vocabulary questions, then ask for three acting volunteers to read the scene in front of the class.

Afterwards, discuss Micah's work with the class. Who are the three characters? How do they relate to one another? How are they similar? How are they different? Based on the first scene, what type of play do students think it will be? (Funny, sad, romantic, adventurous?) Why do they think that? What do they think the play will be about? What do they think will happen next? And what could possibly be Foxwoods' Dilemma?

Reflection: Stories are things that people have shared with one another since the beginning of time. Sometimes stories are biographical, sometimes they are flights of fancy and fiction. They have the power to engage, enrage, motivate and change. They can make people feel, think, hope and wonder. The potential for stories are all around us. And stories come from everywhere.

Follow-Up: This can be done as either homework or as an in-class activity. Have each student choose a character, an event, and a setting – either from the brainstormed list created earlier in the lesson or a new one. (More suggestions are provided below.) Then ask them to write a paragraph about what might happen in their chosen character's story. Once completed, have them pair up and share their original stories with a partner. Emphasize that any one of these could be turned into a play.

Character / Event / Setting Suggestions		
Character		
firefighter	flight attendant	detective
teacher	veterinarian	quality inspector
chef	fortune teller	referee
student	piano tuner	paramedic
choreographer	lifeguard	photographer
Event		
first day at work	lighting a barbecue	discovering a cure
receiving a call	saving a life	worst day ever
finding a clue	Thanksgiving meal	love at 1st sight
meeting a stranger	attending a wake	seeing an old friend
overhearing a lie	taking the plunge	catching a train
Setting		
city street	garden	work place
basement	zoo	graveyard
stadium	concert hall	palace
principal's office	small town	beach
hotel lobby	laboratory	train station

2 Dialogue and Conflict

Review: Briefly, as a class review the differences between plays, movies, and books and who the person is who writes plays – the playwright!

Activity: The One-Minute Play (aka The Sixty-Second Script)

Ask for a show of hands of those who have written a play before. Most likely, nary a hand will be raised. Tell them that will all change because today they will be writing their first play. The play is called the *One-Minute Play*. Why do they think it's called that? Elicit a few answers and usually somebody will come up with the response you are looking for: because that's all the time they have to write it.

Have your students take out a blank piece of paper and a pen/pencil. In the meantime, draw a rectangle on the board to represent the page. Tell students to number the piece of paper down the center of the page starting at the top with the number one. Then skip a couple lines and write number two. Skip a couple lines, write number one again. Skip a couple more lines and write number two, and so on to the end of the page. Model this for them on the board (see figure 1 on next page). Ask, "How many characters do you think will be in this play?" The correct answer is two. Once you see somebody who's finished, pick their paper up, show it to the class and tell them their paper should look similar.

If using unlined paper, I tell them to skip two fingers worth of space between each number.

On the board, directly underneath the number one, write a pre-selected sentence that ends in a fill-in-the-blank line. The sentence should be one that can provoke a conflict.

Examples: *Could you please not _____*

Why are you _____

I'm not going to _____

If you continue to _____

Ask them to copy on their paper what you have written on the board (figure 2 on next page). Again, pick up the paper of a student who has completed this step and tell the group that their page should look similar.

Without writing each line of dialogue down, verbally model for them how the activity will go (see figure 3 for sample dialogue). Afterwards, tell them that it is a simple conversation: 1 says something to 2. 2 responds to 1. Then 1 responds to 2. And so on.

Figure 1

Figure 2

Figure 3

Figure 2 text:
1
I'm really going to have to ask you to _____.
2
1
2
1
2
1
2

Figure 3 text:
1
I'm really going to have to ask you to <u>take your dog with you this time.</u>
2
But I thought you liked The Snugster.
1
Nobody likes Snuggles. He's basically a big drool on four legs.
2
You told me you liked him!
1
Well, that was then.
2
Snuggles has nothing to do with our current situation!
1
If you leave, the dog leaves with you.
2
Oh, believe me, I am leaving.

On Your Mark, Get Set, Go!

They now have sixty seconds to write their play. Their mission is to get to the end of the page. If that means writing short back and forth sentences of "yes" / "no" / "yes" / "no" at one point, then so be it. Just get to the end of the page.

You can either be very strict with the clock or keep an eye on where most students are.

I have a tendency to coach the students throughout the minute, announcing the halfway point, and when there's fifteen seconds left. I remind them that this may not be the best play they'll ever write, but it will be their fastest and their first. I encourage them to go with whatever idea they have and not to censor themselves. There are no wrong answers. Just get to the end of the page.

Often times, they will not all be finished by the end of the minute and yet I do ask for pens and pencils up at that point. I then ask who got to the end of the page. Usually only a few hands will raise, in which case I'll quickly declare, "Bonus fifteen extra seconds begins now!" and instruct those who are done to review or embellish.

With the bonus round over, that's it. Congratulate them as they've officially written their first play.

Partner Share
Have students pair up with a nearby neighbor to read their plays out loud. If Jack's play is read first, he gets to decide if he is 1 or 2. If he chooses 1, then his partner, Sue, reads 2. After they read Jack's play, it's Sue's turn. Same drill. Give all paired students a few minutes to read both plays aloud.

While this is happening, walk around the room and make a mental note of any plays that might be fun to share aloud in front of the whole class.

Ask for a pair of volunteers to read one of their two plays to the class. If hands don't instantly shoot up in the air (though they usually do), choose one of the plays you noticed while walking around the room and have that pair of students come to the front of the room to read the play.

In the first time through of reading a few of these aloud, here are things I look to address, point out and ask questions about:

- **Beginning, Middle and End**
- **Character**
- **Relationship**
- **Language**
- **Setting**
- **Wants**

Beginning, Middle and End
After the volunteers share their play and the audience applauds (it is always useful to review applauding at the end of a performance), ask the class what happened first in the play (beginning). Then what happened next (middle). And lastly, how did it close (end). Every piece of theater, every monologue, every scene has a shape to it. The natural evolution is: something is introduced, something happens, then somehow it comes to a close. Although it seems basic, it is worth reviewing because there are times when a scene will peter out or just go on and on or the middle is underdeveloped or the beginning doesn't properly setup what's to come. Hopefully, your first pair of volunteers will have a definitive end, but if not, ask the class how the scene could end.

Character and Relationship
Ask the class who the characters are in the play. Are there any clues in the dialogue about their job or roles in society? Do the characters seem to know one another? If so, why does it seem that way? If not, why not? Sometimes, it'll be obvious whether they know each other or not. If it isn't, ask the class how the playwright could make it clear that the characters either know one another (e.g., adding names, clarifying context) or how they could make it clear that they don't know one another (adding something like "excuse me, sir/ma'am").

Language
Did the class get a sense of how old the characters are? If so, what gave them that sense? Usually the use of language is key. Language can reveal a great deal about individuals such

as where they come from or how old they are or what their background or education is. Have students take a moment to consider the difference between the phrases "not a thing" and "nuttin". What can audiences learn about characters from the language they use? And how can a writer subtly establish character without hitting the audience over the head or without relying on actors to do all the work for them? Ask students to take the following simple two-line dialogue and revise the language to make character and relationship more clear.

Original
1: Can I help you?
2: No, thank you.

Examples:

Revision with 1 as a younger man and 2 as an older woman
1: Excuse me, ma'am, do you need help with that?
2: My goodness, it is ever so kind of you to offer, young man.

Revision with 1 as an adult and 2 as a kid
1: Would you like me to reach that cereal for you?
2: Mommy says I'm not supposed to talk to strangers!

Setting

Scenes happen somewhere. Ask students where the volunteers' scene takes place. How do they know? If it isn't obvious, how could a setting be suggested? Sometimes, students will give visual suggestions – like in order for the setting to be a school, they may suggest the actor wear a backpack or sit at a desk for the scene. These are valid and useful options, but my advice is: if you want something to be in the play, have a character say it or imply it rather than relying on sets and costumes. A simple line like "I kinda forgot my homework, Mr. Kapoor" instantly suggests school. Dialogue is a playwright's best friend and can help establish a lot. The trick is to not be too obvious when offering clues to the audience.

Wants

Good plays usually set up a character who has some sort of want. Ideally, it's a *big want*. One that would inspire a journey. And be interesting enough to engage an audience for the duration of the show. With these sixty-second scripts, however, any notice of character yearning (big or small) will do. Ask the audience to point out what one of the characters wants in the scene.

I usually cover the six points: 1) **Beginning, Middle and End** 2) **Character** 3) **Relationship** 4) **Language** 5) **Setting** and 6) **Want** using four or five volunteers' plays before moving on to the next activity.

Activity: Adding Essential Stage Directions

Open up a conversation on stage directions. What do students think stage directions are? What could their purpose be?

Vocabulary   **Stage Direction – An instruction in the text of the play.**

Stage directions are usually written in italics or in parenthesis so as not to be confused for dialogue.

Stage directions can help establish:

- **Setting**
  The place and/or time of a scene: *Friendship Junior High School cafeteria, 7:25am.*

- **Action**
  Informing an actor to do something: *CARLOS rips up the letter.*
  Establishing an important visual moment: *A gold coin falls from the sky.*

- **Emphasis**
  Cueing an actor on how to say something: MIA *(angrily)*: Never again!

If it is important to the playwright for an actor to emphasize something that might not be so obvious, the last example above can be a useful method. However, it should be used sparingly so that actors aren't constantly being told how to say a line.

Write the below dialogue used earlier on the board:

1:	Can I help you?
2:	No, thank you.

In pairs, have students take this two-line exchange and add character names and at least three stage directions (one setting, one action, one emphasis) so the context of the dialogue becomes clear. They should not change a single word of the dialogue, however. Give them a few minutes to work on the activity, then call on volunteers to share their scene. Were the stage directions clear to the rest of the class? Did the stage directions help inform the story?

Here's an example to share with them:

> *At the library. GRACE is looking at a book.*
>
> LIBRARIAN (*hisses*):   Can I help you?
>
> *GRACE puts the book down.*
>
> GRACE: No, thank you.
>
> *GRACE quickly exits.*

Activity: Brother, Can You Spare a Dime?

Pick a volunteer, ideally someone that might be good at improvisation. Quickly and quietly, explain to the volunteer so the other students can't hear that you two are going to perform a made-up scene twice. The first time you will ask her for an object and she will give it to you. The second time you perform the scene, you will ask for the object again, but this time no matter what, she should not give it to you. Tell her that in the second scene she shouldn't deny that she has the object nor should she just repeatedly say no to you, instead she must come up with reasons as to why she's not going to give it to you.

> ***Entrances and Exits...***
>
> *If possible, at the top of the improvisation, step outside the classroom so that after the 3-2-1 countdown, the scene begins with your entrance and ends with your exit.*

Ask somebody in the class to lead a countdown to the scene with a "3-2-1-action!" You enter with the first line and be sure to address the student by her name:

Teacher: Hey, Vanessa, would you happen to have <u>a dime</u>?
Vanessa: Sure thing, Ms. Renna, here ya go.

Take the mimed dime or whatever object you decide on, then tell the class that was the end of the scene. Review the scene's **beginning, middle and end; character; relationship; language; setting** and **want** with the class.

The short scene from above has all these things. Then get their feedback on the play they've just witnessed. They may be timid at first, but soon you might hear "it was boring" and/or "it was really short". Eventually, somebody will hopefully respond with exactly what you are looking for. "There was no CONFLICT!!!" So even though a scene might have the six components we've already covered, without conflict there's just no drama.

Vocabulary   **Conflict – The dramatic struggle between two forces or a problem that must be solved.**

Do the scene again, but this time, add conflict. It should build naturally and employ many different tactics. Using the example from above, the teacher could: ask, beg, bargain, barter, reason, guilt, threaten, blackmail. Meanwhile, Vanessa has her own trajectory of active verbs and actions to utilize in raising the stakes. Let this scene build to a dramatic ending and then find a way to either leave with the object or leave after giving up. Here's how the scene might begin:

Teacher: Hey, Vanessa, would you happen to have a dime?

Vanessa: Of course I have a dime, Ms. Renna.

Teacher: That's fantastic, I only need the one.

Vanessa: Nope. Sorry. Bag of gumballs with my name on it waiting for me at the corner shop at 3 o'clock.

Teacher: Please, Vanessa; I wouldn't ask you normally.

Vanessa: This is the fourth time you've asked me for some change this week.

Teacher: Yes, but I paid you back every time.

Vanessa: I'm really beginning to wonder why you need so many dimes.

Teacher: Tell you what... if you give me a dime now, I'll bring you a Susan B. Anthony dollar tomorrow.

Vanessa: But the bag of gumballs could be gone by then.

Teacher: Chewing gum will rot your teeth.

Vanessa: It's my money and I can do whatever I want with it.

Teacher: Oh really. Do you think your mom would give you such a great allowance if she knew you were failing math?

Vanessa: I'm not failing math.

Teacher: You sure about that?

Vanessa: Ms. Renna, I don't think I like what you are implying. If my mother, Principal Troyla, hears about this, I am not sure I could save your job a second time...

> ***Another Option...***
>
> *Instead of somebody asking for an object, consider one of the characters needing permission from the other. First time through, permission is easily granted. Second time through, conflict arises.*

Go for *conflict*. And go for *drama*. Your audience will appreciate it. And feel free to remind them that it is only a play.

Once the second scene is complete, ask the class for feedback. On the board, break down why they thought it was more interesting. Write down all the tactics your character attempted. Get students to name the rising actions in order. Explain to them that not all scenes need (or should) end in high stakes drama, however, they need to end somewhere different from where they started. Also, point out that the character in the improvisation did not go from politely asking to suddenly blackmailing. The scene should build organically and have a natural and believable arc.

Reflection: Review all topics covered today. Ask students to name some of the ingredients that go into writing a play:

- **Dialogue**
- **Stage Directions**
- **Beginning, Middle and End**
- **Character**
- **Relationship**
- **Language**
- **Setting**
- **Wants**
- **Conflict**

Any one of these components on their own, do not a play make, but together, they can make for some fantastic drama.

Follow-Up: Have students each write a short scene (2-3 pages) for two characters. The scene should establish:

1. A clear character relationship
2. A clear want
3. A clear conflict
4. A clear setting
5. A clear beginning, middle and end
6. And three relevant stage directions

3   Plot Sequencing

Review: Brainstorm as a class, the list of the play components you've covered so far:

Dialogue	Stage Directions	Beginning, Middle & End
Character	Relationships	Language
Setting	Wants	Conflict

Have the class think back to Micah's play, *The Foxwoods Dilemma* (worksheet B). Ask for examples of how Micah used these play components in his opening scene. Review the beginning, middle and end play component last, as it will serve as a transition to the next activity.

Warm-Up: No Narrator Needed

Read a Tale
Choose a short fable, myth or legend (ideally only one or two paragraphs long) that is appropriate for your students' age group, has more than one character, and is a bit obscure so that your students are not necessarily familiar with it. Feel free to find your own piece or use the one below. (For younger students, consider using the folk tale, *Stone Soup*, for this activity.)

> **The Belly and the Members** by Aesop
>
> One fine day it occurred to the Members of the Body that they were doing all the work and the Belly was having all the food. So they held a meeting, and after a long discussion, decided to go on strike till the Belly agreed to take its proper share of the work. For a day or two, the Hands refused to take the food, the Mouth refused to receive it, and the Teeth had no work to do. But after a day or two the Members began to find that they themselves were not in a very active condition: the Hands could hardly move, and the Mouth was all parched and dry, while the Legs were unable to support the rest. So thus they found that even the Belly, in its dull quiet way, was doing necessary work for the Body, and that they all must work together or the Body will go to pieces.

Read the story out loud once, then ask students to name all the characters in the story while you write their responses on the board.

    Characters: Belly, Hands, Mouth, Teeth, Legs

Break It Down

Now ask them to name the *significant events* of the story. Discuss the difference between significant events and other events so that students provide only the major moments of the piece. Deliberately write their responses on the board in the incorrect story sequence order.

Significant Events: The strike, the withering away, the members realize unfairness, the members' meeting, the members' second realization

Read the story again and see if there are any other characters or significant events that were left out.

Ask a volunteer to reorder the events on the board so that they are in the correct order and to also put a **B**, **M**, or **E** for beginning, middle, or end in front of each event for when each event happens in the story:

- **B**: The members realize unfairness
- **B**: The members' meeting
- **M**: The members' strike
- **M**: The members' withering away
- **E**: The members' second realization

Act It Out I (with narrator)

Request volunteers to play the five characters. This time you will read the story out loud and the five volunteers will act it out without speaking a single word. When you read it, be sure to pause throughout your narration so that the performers have sufficient time to act out their part.

Get the audience's feedback to this version of the story.

Act It Out II (without narrator)

Now have the same group of volunteers – or a new set of five volunteers – act out the entire story using their own *dialogue* and *action* without any narration from you. Tell them it is their job to hit all the bullet points of the beginning, middle and end and to tell the story in order. Give them a "3-2-1-action!" and let them loose.

Afterwards, get the audience's feedback. How did the story change without a narrator? Were the actors able to convey the story through dialogue and action alone? Although many stories use narration, it is seldom used in plays. Encourage them to avoid unnecessary narration when it comes to their own playwriting.

Activity: Plot Sequencing

Hand out copies of the *Plot Diagram* (worksheet C) or copy the diagram below on the board:

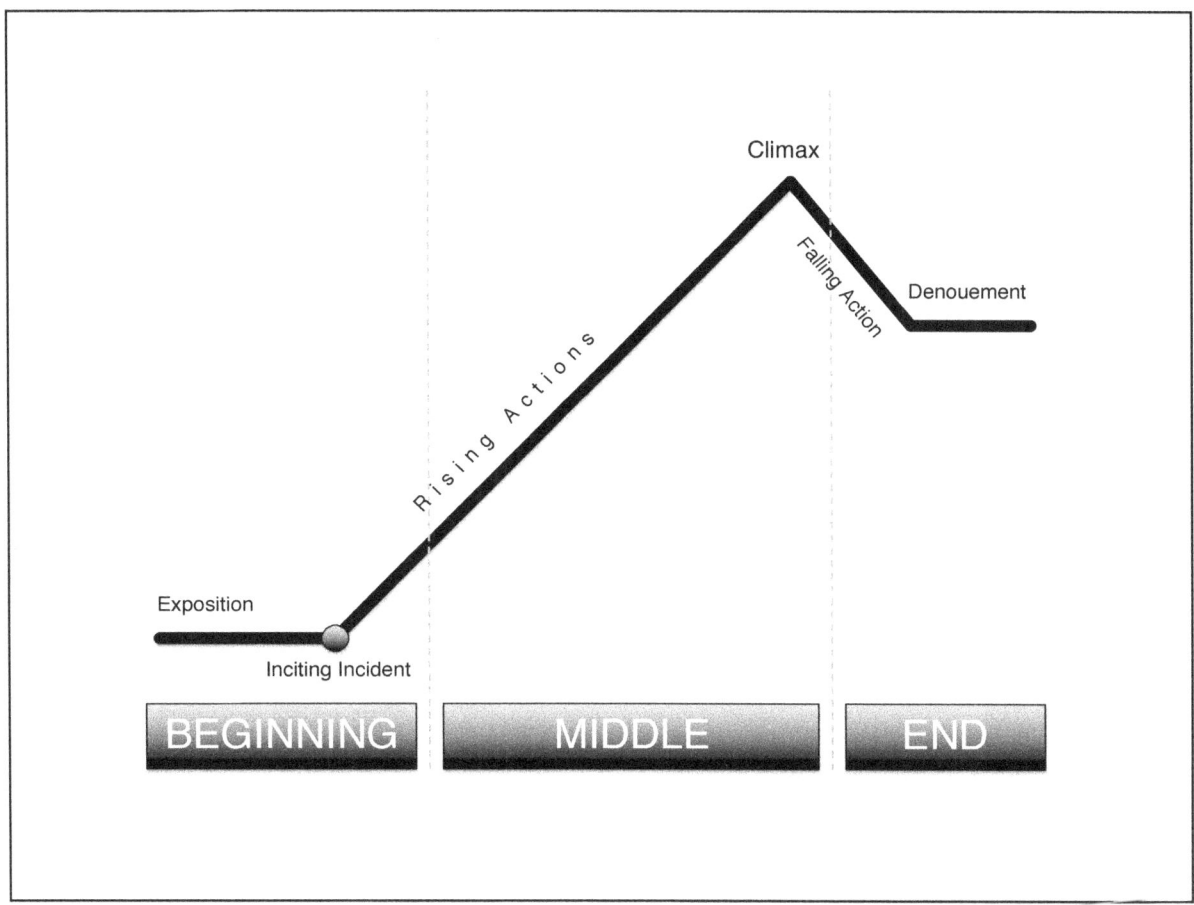

Tell students this is a map of a play. It's not the only way to map out a play, but this is the one we will use for our purposes. Ask them, "Based on this map, can you tell where most of the time of a play is spent?" The middle is the correct answer. The middle of a story represents the peanut butter and jelly while the beginning and ending are the two pieces of bread that hold it all together.

There are other words on the map that may be new concepts for some students. Take a moment to define these words and give examples using a story that students are familiar with. I shall use *Little Red Riding Hood.*

Exposition
In *Little Red Riding Hood,* we meet the main character, Little Red, who lives near the edge of the woods, always wears a red cape and has a grandmother who lives through the woods.

Vocabulary   **Exposition – The beginning part of a play that gives important background information on character and situation.**

Inciting Incident

Grandmother becomes ill so Mother sends Little Red with a basket of goodies to take to Grandmother. (If Grandmother doesn't get sick, then there would be no need for Little Red to go through the forest and the Wolf would never have had the chance to meet her. Without the inciting incident, the story doesn't happen!)

Vocabulary   **Inciting Incident –** **The event that jumpstarts the action of the play (after the exposition).**

Rising Actions

Little Red meets the Wolf and she tells him where she is going. Then the Wolf runs ahead of her and eats her Grandmother. Then the Wolf climbs into bed and pretends to be Grandmother just as Little Red Riding Hood arrives and questions why Grandmother looks different.

Vocabulary   **Rising Action –** **A series of events following the inciting incident that develops conflict and/or character and leads up to the climax of the play.**

Climax

The Wolf removes the disguise. Will he eat Little Red Riding Hood? Yes, he will – and does!

Vocabulary   **Climax – The turning point or high point of the story.**

Falling Action

The Wolf, now satiated, falls asleep and begins to snore. A Hunter hears the snoring, enters and sees the Wolf in Grandmother's bed.

Vocabulary   **Falling Action –** **The series of events that happen after the climax.**

Denouement

The Hunter cuts the Wolf's belly open releasing Little Red and Grandmother. Everybody, but the Wolf, lives *happily ever after*.

Vocabulary   **Denouement – The conclusion or resolution of the play (French for "unraveling").**

As a group, plot out your selected story on the *Plot Diagram* worksheet:

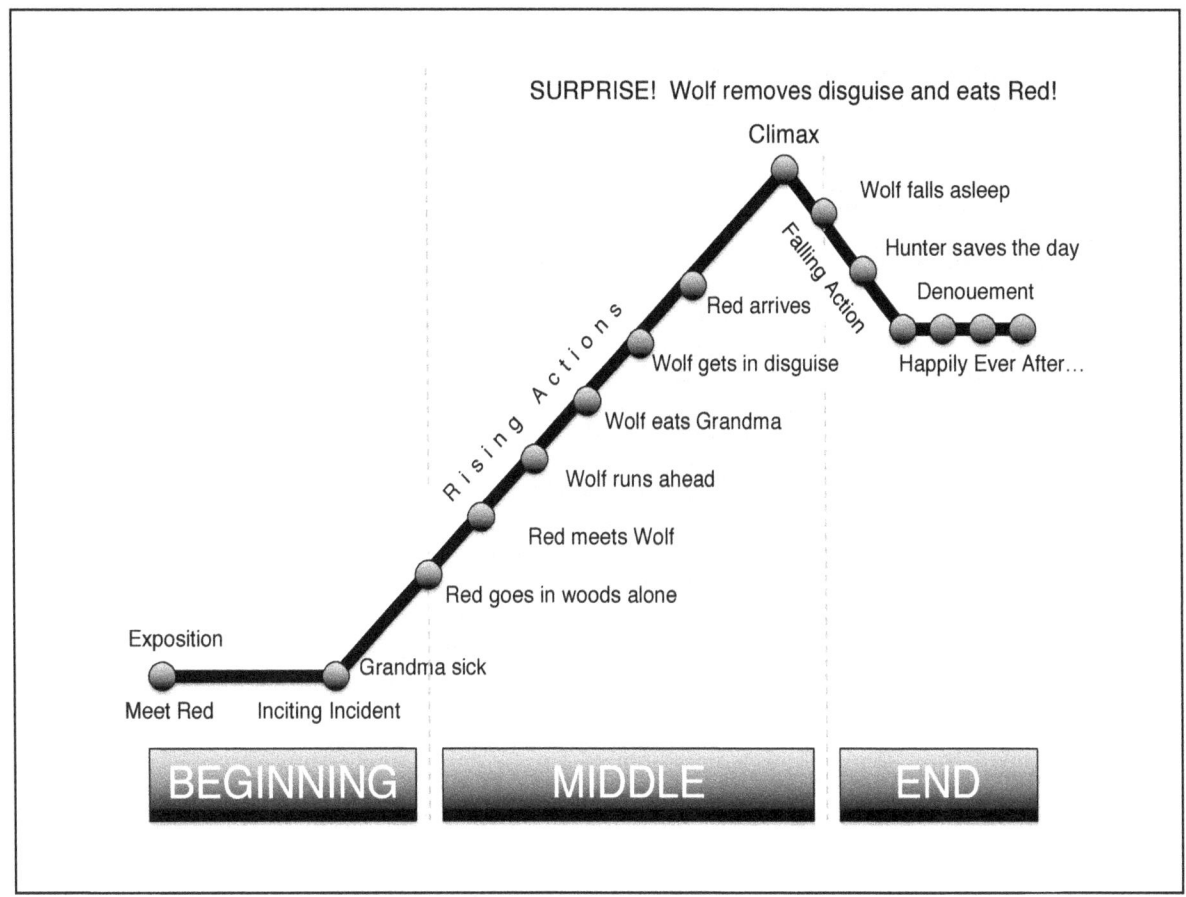

Activity: Name that Tale

Give students one minute to write down the titles of as many fairytales and/or folktales as they can. Once time is up, elicit the titles to write on the board. Some suggestions:

- *Beauty and the Beast*
- *Cinderella*
- *The Emperor's New Clothes*
- *Goldilocks & the Three Bears*
- *Hansel and Gretel*
- *Jack and the Beanstalk*

- *Little Red Riding Hood*
- *The Little Mermaid*
- *The Princess & the Pea*
- *Rapunzel*
- *Rip Van Winkle*
- *Rumpelstiltskin*

- *Sleeping Beauty*
- *The Snow Queen*
- *Snow White*
- *Stone Soup*
- *Three Little Pigs*
- *The Ugly Duckling*

If you are working on a particular unit of study (creation myths, trickster stories, world tales) you can tailor this and the following activity to said unit.

Activity: Plot that Tale

In groups of four, have each team select one of the tales listed on the board. If you have butcher paper and markers, hand them out, otherwise regular paper will suffice.

Each team's mission is to:

- Break down their story into a minimum of *nine* significant events
- Map the events out onto a plot diagram

Each team's map must include the following nine points:

1. Exposition
2. Inciting Incident
3. Rising Action #1
4. Rising Action #2
5. Rising Action #3
6. Rising Action #4
7. Climax
8. Falling Action
9. Denouement

Give them ten minutes to discuss and map. When everyone is done, have each team present their map to the rest of the class. Each student must be responsible for at least two items in the presentation. You can give them an additional five minutes to prepare their presentation. Gauge this based on need. Although rising actions may vary, be sure to double check their inciting incident and climax just to verify they are on track of understanding what sets the story in motion and how the action peaks.

If time allows, give them a bonus activity. Have students list how their fairytale incorporates or could incorporate: **dialogue, stage directions, beginning, middle and end, character, relationship, language, setting, wants,** and **conflict.**

Reflection: Maps are guides that help us navigate the world. Likewise, a plot diagram map helps us chart out the world of a play. We just read a story and created a map of its arc. Next, we will do the reverse – create a map and then write the story.

Follow-Up: Have students copy down the following open-ended sentence and come up with a minimum of six unique ways to finish it.

*Wouldn't it be amazing if*_____

Example: *Wouldn't it be amazing if <u>kids ruled the world?</u>*

Encourage them to think outside the box and really go for something awe-inspiring. Any one of the ideas from this short list has the potential to be turned into a play at a later point.

4   Creating Character I – from a Photo

Do Now: What Makes You, You?

As students trickle in, have the phrase "What Makes You, You?" written on the board. Ask them to come up with five things that make them who they are. The list can range from physical traits to biographical facts, anything that is specific to them and would help a stranger learn a bit about them.

> **Examples**:   1. *freckles on my nose*
> 2. *a birthmark shaped like Africa on my leg*
> 3. *a younger brother who drives me crazy*
> 4. *a love of math*
> 5. *can never remember jokes*

Have students circle one attribute that they would like to read out loud, then share a few examples. When there is a trait that could apply to many students (e.g., *I have brown hair*), ask other students who have brown hair to raise their hands. While having them keep their hands up, ask the original brown haired student for another attribute on their list (e.g., *plays the piano*). Now ask those students with hands raised to keep their hands up if they also play the piano. A number of hands will most likely go down. Ask the original brown haired piano player for another attribute (e.g., *has a scar on knee*). Ask the remaining students with their hands raised to keep their hands up if, in addition to brown hair and piano playing skills, they also have a scar on their knee. Keep going until there is nobody left with his or her hand raised except for the original brown-haired, piano-playing, scarred-knee student.

Let them know that: "*These are just some of the things that make you, you. Every one of you is an individual and even though you may share some similarities, no two people are exactly alike.*" Follow up by telling students that today they are going to create a character who is a unique individual just like they are.

Activity: Looking Exercise

Tell students this next activity is a *Looking Exercise*. Show them a photo of a person and instruct students to take in as much of the image as possible. This is a silent activity that should be guided by your voice only. While you slowly walk around the room, show the image to everybody and prompt them with some key observations to notice.

Prompt Examples:
- Notice what the person is wearing.
- Notice what is in the background.
- Notice what is in the foreground.
- Notice what clues are in the photo.
- Notice whether there is a sense of time period.
- Notice any details about the weather.
- Notice whether there is a sense of place.
- Notice what the mood of the person appears to be.
- Notice something that maybe nobody else notices.

Offer the above prompts and more like them until every student has the opportunity to take in the picture.

Advice on Choosing Active Images

A good photo to me is one that tells a story. Active images are evocative, rich, candid, and have a sense of mood. Ideally there is some sort of setting that helps give the photo context. The pictures can include characters who are gritty and hard or innocent and enchanting. What's important is that the image should have characters who have a story to tell. I tend to use images with only one person in the picture so the focus is on that one key person. I am always on the lookout for interesting character photos and I recommend that you start a collection of your own. Most pictures I use are cut out of magazines. I then put them on colored cardstock and laminate them. This way, they can be used over and over again and remain in good condition. Magazines that I like to collect inspiration from include: *The New Yorker, Harpers, National Geographic, Inc., New York Times Magazine, Time,* and *Scientific American*, to name but a few. Often, the more inspiring photos come from very unassuming magazines (think entrepreneurial magazines or independent quarterlies). I avoid all celebrity, glamour, fashion, entertainment and sports magazines as students' characters will likely end up as pretty people who want to be models or famous. There is, I believe, a place for one or two of these characters to crop up, but I rather encourage students to create a character of a young woman who wants to be an astronaut over a young woman who wants to be known for being pretty. I tend to avoid photos of people posing directly for the camera or people who are advertising products, and images with words splayed across them. Websites such as flickr.com/commons or commons.wikimedia.org are useful because as they offer sections with photos in the public domain. Some photographers I look to for inspiration include: Vivian Maier, Damon Casarez (*Boomerang Kids* series) and Joel Meyerowitz. I've also found a number of worthwhile examples by doing an online image keyword search of "environmental portrait photography", "candid portraiture" and "street photography".

Activity: The Eight W's of Character Development (Part I)

After students have observed the photo, ask for suggestions on (1) **WHO** is this character? What is their first name? Their last name? Any nicknames? Move on to age. (2) **WHAT AGE** do they think the character is? (3) **WHERE** is the character? (4) **WHEN** does this scene take place? Write these biographical details on the board.

Elicit detailed answers using the above questions. For WHERE, "somewhere in Europe" is a good start, but get students to be specific. Aim for a more detailed answer like, "in Vladimir's living room in Grebbestad, a fishing village in Sweden near the Norwegian border". For WHEN, "March 4th, 1998 on Vladimir's birthday" is a clearer picture than "in the 90s".

> *What's in a Name?*
>
> *The first thing our character needs is a name. A name that would suit them. If I have a photo of an Eastern European-looking man, I'll ask students what his name would probably not be. Blake. Spencer. Billy Bob. Then we discuss why it most likely wouldn't be any of those. It's not to say an Eastern-European man couldn't be called Juan Jose, but unless an incongruous name is part of the story, then it may be a red herring that confuses an audience. I also ask students to stay away from clearly famous names or anybody's name in the classroom.*

Next ask: (5) **WHAT DOES HE/SHE WANT?** Before taking suggestions, tell them to put their hands down. This is their opportunity to envisage a character who has *big wants* as opposed to everyday wants.

Examples:
- In *The Little Mermaid*, Ariel wants to be human.
- In *The Lion King*, Simba wants to be king.
- In *The Wizard of Oz*, Dorothy wants to go home.
- In *Annie*, Annie wants to find her family.

It is these big wants – these universal wants – that can help drive a play. And big wants will hopefully inspire big ideas. So while "wanting a cup of coffee" or "wanting a manicure" are solid, regular wants, a big want is one that can propel a character on a significant journey.

So... ask your students for some big wants for the character you are all creating together:

Examples: Vladimir Ivanavich wants:
- to be successful
- to find love
- to return to his homeland
- to attain inner peace

As a group, agree on one main, overarching want. It's not to say that a person can't want more than one thing in life (we are all multi-faceted beings), but so that your scenario is focused, hone in on a particular one. In Vladimir Ivanavich's case, let's say he wants to return to his homeland.

After asking WHAT DOES HE/SHE WANT? move on to the last three questions: (6) ***WHY DOES HE/SHE WANT IT?*** (7) ***WHAT DOES HE/SHE DO TO GET IT?*** and (8) ***WHO OR WHAT GETS IN HIS/HER WAY?***

Questions 7 and 8 can and should have multiple answers. You would never have a character only try one thing and then give up, that wouldn't make for a very interesting story. A character needs to be presented with a variety of hurdles to overcome and different ways to overcome them.

Tada! In a short amount of time, you have all created a rich character with a backstory and a big want. Sometimes, I'll ask students to come up with possible scenes for this play. Who would be in them and what would be the main crux of the scene?

Examples:
- The scene where Vladimir (in Sweden) learns that his sister (in Bulgaria) is sick.
- The scene where Vladimir and his Swedish wife, Astrid, get into a "discussion" over his wanting to leave.
- The scene where Vladimir's train ticket (and wallet) is stolen and so he has to find another way to get to Bulgaria.
- The scene where Vladimir is confronted by the Bulgarian Border Patrol for trying to enter the country without proper papers.
- The scene where Vladimir is at his sister's bedside.

In my experience, occasionally somebody will suggest a negative action for the character either in jest or for real. I always take the opportunity to discuss protagonist choices. If Vladimir suddenly joins a gang and mugs an innocent person, then the audience has a harder time sympathizing with him. We should want audiences to care for our characters and root for them.

> **Poor Character Choices and the Likability Factor**
>
> In the television show, *The Office,* there is an episode where the boss, Michael, goes to an improvisation class. Whenever he is in an improv, he pulls out a pretend gun. The other characters are forced to then be victims or the only other choice is for them to pull out a pretend gun, too. These sorts of scenes rarely use words, which are the playwright's tools, but rather impending violence. And where can a scene really go once a gun is introduced? It is a potentially dangerous path. I will never limit a student's creativity, but I will challenge them as a playwright to use their words first and foremost. I will also challenge them to find a way to get the audience on the character's side. Jean Valjean in *Les Misérables* steals a loaf of bread, but he's not a bad guy; he did it to feed his sister's starving children. My advice: keep protagonists likeable.

Activity: A House Is Not a Home

In the back of the book (worksheets E and F) there are pictures of two houses. Make a copy of each picture or use the originals. House A is very basic whereas House B is very intricate. Show your students a picture of House A. Ask them what it is. They will easily shout out "a house". Now show them a picture of House B. Repeat the question. Their answers will vary from "a better house" to "a home". Ask what the difference is between the two houses. You may hear one is 2-D and one is 3-D, which is technically not true as both are 2-D. But what is it that makes the second house appear to be 3-D? Invariably, someone will have the answer you're looking for: *The Details.*

Students can create a character sketch like the basic house or they can create one like the detailed house. Which do they think the audience would find more interesting? An audience doesn't need to necessarily know where the drainpipes are or whether there are sash or casement windows, but the playwright – like an architect – should be able to address the blueprints.

Activity: The Eight W's of Character Development (Part II)

Now, it's your students' turn to create a character from a photo. Hand out an individual photo to each student and *The Eight W's of Character Development* (worksheet D).

Give them 5-7 minutes to work on the character worksheet. I always tell students that the first four questions should be answered swiftly as they can always go back and adjust if necessary. It is the second half of the worksheet where they ought to spend the bulk of their time.

While they are working I walk around and see if there are any questions. I also glance at the first four answers to make sure adequate details are being provided. However, I mainly focus on checking their answer for "What does he/she want?"

If a student has something written like "she wants a flower", I will challenge them to make the want "bigger" and more universal. This way, they will have more to mine for in their play. Additionally – though less important – a more universal topic may be more relatable to a wider audience.

The conversation might go something like this:

    You: Why does she want a flower?
    Student: Because she likes them.
    You: Why does she like them?
    Student: Because she thinks they're pretty.
    You: Why does she want pretty things?
    Student: Because she never had them growing up.

Eureka! Suddenly "she wants a flower" becomes "she wants to be surrounded by beauty" or "she wants to forget her childhood". These revised statements of want have the potential for a richer story arc than a character who just wants a daisy because she likes flowers.

After the students are done with their worksheet, have them pair up and share with a partner. They should take turns introducing their character out loud to their partner as opposed to just exchanging their paper and picture. The listening partner should feel free to ask questions if any come up.

Afterwards, ask for volunteers who are willing to introduce their characters to the class.

Reflection: The woman who works as a financial advisor, the man who runs the tilt-a-whirl at the carnival – they are not just their jobs, that is just one aspect of who they are. They have dreams, inspirations, and wants. They have a past and a hope for the future. Your characters have the potential to be as real as the people of this world. And it is all in the details.

Follow-Up: Come up with three possible scenes for your character's story. List who else would be in the scene and what the scene would be about.

5 Creating Character II – from Random Props

Warm-Up: Parts of the Stage

Plays happen live on a stage. A stage can be traditional, like one you would find in a school auditorium. Or it can be non-traditional, as in an adjustable black box space or a parking lot or the front of your classroom.

Tell your students to imagine that the first row of desks is the first row of an audience and that the space between the first row and the blackboard is the stage.

Choose a volunteer (V1) to come up on stage and stand **center stage**. Ask the class, "Do you agree that V1 is center stage?" If so, move on. If not, have her adjust using the class' input so that she is in the center.

Get a second volunteer (V2) to stand next to V1. While V1 remains center stage, ask V2 to stand **center right**. Ask the audience if V2 appears to be standing in the correct position. There may be a bit of confusion, because the audience's right is different from the actor's right. Take a moment to explain that the stage is oriented from the *actor's point of view*, not the audience's point of view. While it may look like V2 is standing to the left of V1, he is actually standing stage right of her.

Have a third volunteer (V3) join V1 and V2 on stage. Ask V3 to stand **center left**. Your three volunteers should be standing as illustrated:

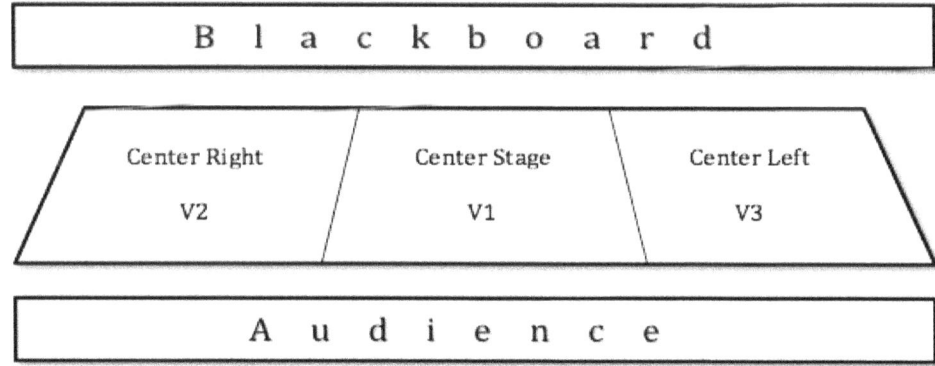

Go through the other six areas of a stage (see image on the next page) as six more volunteers come up one at a time. Describe how most stages used to be raked at an angle so that the back of the stage was slightly higher than the front. The front of the stage was therefore called **down center** while the higher, further back part of the stage was known as **up center**. The four remaining areas are called: **down left**, **down right**, **up left** and **up right**.

Once all nine volunteers are in place, have them move around the stage while you call out "Simon Says" type directions.

Examples:
- *Sean, please cross from center right to down left.*
- *Jazzmin, please move from up left to center stage.*
- *All non-sneakered volunteers gather down right.*

Ask the audience to provide additional stage direction suggestions.

Reinforce the parts of a stage, by drawing this illustration on the board:

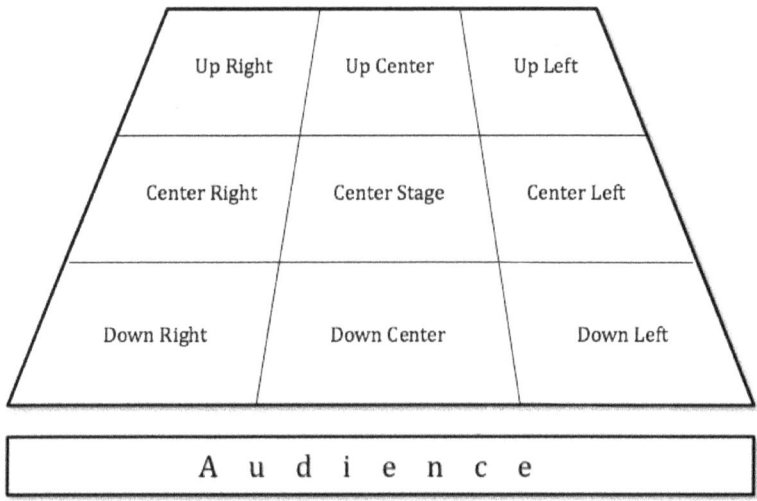

Activity: Props in the Box

What is a prop? Have a class discussion about what a prop is in real life and what a prop might be in theater. Probe ideas from the class. Eventually, write the definition of the word on the board.

Vocabulary   **Prop – A portable object that is used on the set of a play.**

Instruct students to tear a sheet of paper into three strips. Do this activity with them. Then place three boxes at the front of the classroom: one at stage right, one at center stage, and one at stage left.

On the first strip of paper, have students write down something in their house that holds special meaning to them. Ask them to then fold the piece of paper and put it in the stage right box.

Example: a black feather

Side Coaching...

Urge students to pick items that are smaller than a breadbox, hence portable. Having to work with "the toenail of an elephant" might actually warrant some more interesting options than an "elephant" itself might.

On the second strip of paper, have students write down something that is in the classroom right now that nobody else might notice, then fold the paper and put it in the stage left box.

> **Example:**   a dustpan with a broken handle

For the third strip of paper, have them think of an interesting profession (not sports or music related) and write down one item required for said profession, then fold the paper and put it in the center box.

> **Example:**   a compass

Have three volunteers come up and mix the strips of paper. Direct each volunteer to their designated box using stage directions covered in the warm-up.

> **Example:**   *Karly, can you please mix the paper in the stage right box.*

Ask a new volunteer to come up and pick one slip from each box and read each item out loud. Together as a class, create a character who would own these three items.

After completing this as a group, move on to individual work.

Activity: Creating a Character from a Random Prop List

Have every student pick one slip from each box so that they have a random set of three props. If they pick one of their own that is fine.

Their task is to create a character who is the sort of person who would own these three disparate items, which have come to be of some importance in their life. If they manage to connect the three items, even better, but it is not necessary. Give them 5-7 minutes to create a name for their character and a short paragraph that begins with the following statement:

> **Do Now:**   __(Character's name)__ *is the kind of person who…*

Ask them to underline their character's name as well as the three items.

> **Example A:**   __***Adelaide Witherspoon***__ *is the kind of person who gets lost in life easily, but doesn't like people to know that, so she secretly carries a __**compass**__ and checks it out when people aren't looking. She grew up surrounded by nature and beauty, but now lives in a cold city and so she always wears a __**feather**__ in her hair to remind her of from where she came. When she first moved to the city, she worked in a factory that made dustpans and on her last day there, they gave her a company __**dustpan**__ as a joke, which made her furious. When she came home, she threw it against the wall and broke the handle and she promised herself*

that she would never get stuck in a job doing something she didn't want to do ever again.

Example B: *__Julian Smith-Baymore__ is the kind of person who doesn't like to take no for an answer, which is why he wears a __"say yes" button__ on the lapel of his jacket. He's a patriotic sort of man who firmly believes in America and what it stands for. And to show his patriotism, he's attached a small __American flag__ to his car's antenna. Although he's a car salesman and hands out his __business card__ whenever he gets the chance, he has high hopes of one day running for office.*

Have students share their character sketches with a partner. They should read their paragraph out loud to their partner and then actively listen when it's their partner's turn.

Do their characters share any similarities? If so, what? If not, what attributes might they have in common? Would their characters know one another? If so, how? If not, how could they meet?

Activity: Generating Scenarios

Ask paired up students to generate three different scenarios that could occur between their two characters. If they can use one or more of their items to help with a possible story line, all the better.

Example 1: *Julian decides to run for a local board position, but he feels he needs to work on his "likeability factor" and so he puts an ad in the paper for a "life coach who is good with people". Adelaide, looking for a new line of work, decides to respond to the ad.*

Example 2: *Free-spirited Adelaide is protesting against the tearing down of a local park to build a car dealership when she runs into Julian, a former colleague from her dustpan factory days, who is now in charge of the project.*

Example 3: *Julian finds a compass in the park that is engraved with the words, "please find me" on the back of it and so he goes in search of the owner of the compass.*

As they write, remind students to come up with three entirely different ideas for possible stories, not three inter-related ideas. More ideas mean more options from which to choose.

Call on a few volunteers to share their characters and possible scenarios with the class. Provide helpful feedback and ask class for positive and encouraging feedback.

Example: *What did you like about the park versus dealership storyline?*

Reflection: You have just created a character and three scenarios out of nothing more than a few props and your imagination. Although a blank page can sometimes seem like a scary white monster, all you need if you are ever stuck is an inspirational idea to get you started. Ideas can come from anywhere. They can come from pictures, from newspaper headlines, from stories passed down through familial generations, and they can even come from a random list of props that you have at home or in the classroom or from your imagination.

Follow-Up: Have each student write a two-page scene from one of the three scenarios they generated with their partner. In order not to end up with similar storylines, each student should choose a different scenario. After they've completed their written scene, have them also note three possible further scenes for their character's story. Additionally, if you have not done session four's *Creating Character from a Photo*, have students complete *The Eight W's of Character Development* (worksheet D) for the character they created today.

6   Creating Character III – from Improvisation

It's invigorating and creatively freeing for students to sometimes get out of their seats to move around, so this session is dedicated to on-your-feet improvisation. Once students have the basis for a character through this method, they can always fill in the biographical information as they would in the lesson on *Creating Character from a Photo*, but for now, it's time to move the desks to the edge of the room so that there is some space to move around.

Warm-Up: Exploring Space and Movement

Instruct students to mill around the room at a regular pace while respecting other people's personal space. Challenge them to also be aware of their own personal space so that they don't accidentally (or perhaps purposefully) bump into others. Encourage them to use the entire open space. If the middle of the room becomes congested, suggest that they walk elsewhere.

This warm-up works really well with music as it loosens inhibitions and can change the way students choose to move. If you can play music in the classroom, go for it.

Direct students to freeze in place whenever you stop the music or when you call out, "freeze". This, in itself, is a good way for them to practice following directions. You can then ask them to change direction or vary their walking pace until the next "freeze" is called out.

After they've successfully implemented the freeze-then-walk combination, begin to call out other types of locomotive movement.

Vocabulary   **Locomotive Movement – Movement through space.**

       Example: *skipping, galloping, zigzagging, snaking, sliding, shuffling*

Feel free to be creative with your instructions.

       Example: *skip in a straight line, gallop on the diagonal, robot on abrupt right angles, slither lazily to your left*

Once various locomotive movements have been explored, introduce axial movement with a question. "What sort of movement can you do by staying in place?"

Vocabulary   **Axial Movement – Movement in a fixed place.**

       Example: *flick, turn, wiggle, melt, radiate, spin, contract, wave*

Switch between locomotive and axial movement so that students get practice doing both.

Activity: Exploring Shapes and Levels

After exploring space and movement, it's time to add another layer: shapes and levels. Instruct students to once again mill around the room, but this time when you say "freeze", they should make a shape with their body. Any shape is fine as long as they can hold this shape for at least three seconds without moving.

Most likely, in the beginning the shapes they've chosen will look rather neutral or small. Encourage them to take up space using their entire body so that they are really exaggerating and utilizing their extremities.

Next time you stop the music, tell them to freeze on a high level. What does that mean to them? How high can they get and still be able to hold it for three seconds? What different shapes can they make at that level? Then direct a low level freeze, followed by a middle level freeze, each time breaking it up with either locomotive movement or axial movement.

Their three levels – high, medium and low – should be specific and distinct. Encourage students to be bold with both their levels and shapes. Do a rapid fire call out of various levels to get them away from pre-thinking their shapes.

> **Example:** *high shape, low shape, low shape, low shape, mid shape*

Begin to add expressive adjectives to the call-outs.

> **Example:** *a proud high shape*
> *a terrifying low shape*
> *a sweet middle shape*

Take a moment to point out a few examples. Perhaps Maggie's "proud shape" is particularly proud. Ask Maggie to hold her pose while the rest of the class takes a closer look as if they are walking around an art gallery and Maggie is a sculpture for them to observe and appreciate. Ask them questions that could start to suggest a story. "Why is Maggie's character so proud?" "What do you think her character accomplished today that makes her so proud?" "Who else do you think would be in the scene at this moment?" If they suggest her mother, ask, "Can somebody join in as her mother at a different level and cheer Maggie on?"

Expressive Adjectives...				
-happy	*-silly*	*-unsure*	*-relaxed*	*-wild*
-sad	*-excited*	*-bored*	*-secretive*	*-annoyed*
-proud	*-shocked*	*-calm*	*-scary*	*-simple*
-defiant	*-mysterious*	*-nervous*	*-friendly*	*-carefree*
-angry	*-fabulous*	*-suspicious*	*-graceful*	*-polite*

Continue with some more shapes and level combinations while pointing out a few more examples. If you happen to notice two students' shapes relating to one another, take the opportunity to highlight this observation.

Activity: Mini-Share

As they should be quite comfortable with levels, shapes, movement and space by now, give students five minutes in groups of 5 or 6 to put together a mini-performance to share with the class. Their short performance should include the below six steps in order. Although they have freedom to pose differently from one another in the shape sections, they are to perform each movement section in unison (e.g., they all sashay or they all melt).

1. Locomotive Movement
2. Shape 1
3. Axial Movement
4. Shape 2
5. Locomotive Movement
6. Shape 3

Once rehearsed, have each group share their work. As a class, review what methods were employed after each presentation.

Activity: Putting It All Together and Tableau

Ask for two volunteers to stand in front of the class. Then tell them they will be creating a tableau.

Vocabulary   **Tableau – A frozen picture representing a moment in time.**

Let them know that the shapes they just performed in small groups were essentially tableaux. Make sure everybody is comfortable with saying the word and write it on the board so that they see the spelling of it.

From the rest of the class, get two suggestions of levels and two suggestions of expressive shapes.

    Example: *a high level and a middle level*
                      a silly shape and an annoyed shape

Ask the two volunteers to create a tableau with one person representing one of the suggested levels and shapes and the other person taking on the other suggested level and shape. Also, they must establish a relationship with each other in the tableau, as they are not in this picture alone. Give them five seconds to quickly decide who will take on what shape and level, and then have the rest of the class count them down.

Call-out: *3 – 2 – 1 – TABLEAU!*

While the two volunteers are frozen, ask the class to make some observations about the tableau. Which volunteer took on which shape and level combination? Does it look like the characters created by the volunteers know each other? What does the story seem to be? Where could these two characters be? What could they be doing? If each character had one line to speak, what might that line be?

Then have everyone get into small groups of 3 or 4. Give them a few minutes to come up with a group tableau based on a specific setting. Brainstorm a list of places to get them started.

Example: *restaurant, hospital, schoolyard, car dealership, camp, the mall, spaceship, the beach, a cornfield, waiting room*

Each tableau must have:

- a specific setting
- three different levels
- three distinct expressive shapes
- a cohesive visual story

Once the prep time is over, give groups a bonus two minutes to come up with a single spoken line for each character. Then have groups each share their tableau with the rest of the class. Use the call-out "3-2-1-Tableau" to have them transition from neutral to tableau.

Can the class guess the story or setting or any of the character relationships in each tableau? If it's still a mystery, have the group add their individual lines of dialogue. Did that make things clearer? What might happen next in the story?

Reflection: Through improvisation and physical exploration, each student created a character that was a part of a bigger story.

Follow-Up: Have each student write a paragraph about the story of their tableau from their character's point of view, as well as three possible scenes if this story turned into a larger piece. Have them write down specific details of the event including how their character fits in the story. Additionally, if you have not done the lesson on *Creating Character from a Photo*, have students complete *The Eight W's of Character Development* (worksheet D) using the character they created today.

7 The Monologue

Review: Take a moment to go over the character work that students have done so far. No matter what method was used to create a character, students should have a firm grasp and be able to easily answer questions about their character.

Warm-Up: Talk for a Minute

Speaking as Themselves
Have students pair up for this activity. One student is "A" and the other is "B". Each student has one minute to speak on a given topic. Their mission is to stay on topic to the best of their ability and to talk for the entire sixty seconds without stopping.

If A goes first, B's job is to listen and keep track of A's speech habits. Does A pause a lot? Use "ums" and "ahs" repeatedly? Are there words she repeats more than others?

Once the minute is up, it is now B's turn to speak on a different topic and A's turn to listen and pay attention to B's habits.

After the second minute is up and both partners have spoken, open a discussion up on what students noticed about their experience when speaking to and observing their partner. Was this a hard/easy activity? Why? Were they able to stay on topic?

Speaking as a Character
Tell them that they are going to do this exercise once more, but this time, they will speak in the voice of a given character. To prompt them, you will provide part of their first sentence. This time B will start and the character they must voice is either a king or a queen. Write on the board the beginning of their first line and give them one minute to speak.

> **Example**: *As king/queen of this great nation of ours and all its people, I feel it is my duty to discuss...*

You can either give them the topic or let them choose. After the minute is up, it's A's turn again. Give them a completely different character. Here's a possible first line prompt:

> **Example**: *So I said to her, "I may be a slow-witted giant with a nasally voice, but there isn't a thing I don't know about..."*

Possible Topics...

- volleyball	- chores	- school lunch	- the letter "M"	- school safety	- respect
- eggs	- herbs & spices	- worms	- rainbows	- normalcy	- peer pressure
- summertime	- camping	- water	- recycling	- dreaming big	- cyberbullying
- air balloons	- the circus	- ghosts	- the moon	- goodness	- acceptance

If they are able to stay on task without laughing, kudos to them!

Once again, discuss the experience as a class. Was it harder speaking as a character as opposed to speaking as themselves? Easier? Why? Did their use of language change when speaking as royalty or a slow-witted giant? How? How could this activity help us when writing for our characters?

Introduce: Monologues

Ask students, "How many people speak in a dialogue?"

Vocabulary   **Dialogue – A conversation between two people or more.**

Once correctly answered, move on to "How many people do you think speak in a monologue?"

Vocabulary   **Monologue – A speech made by one actor.**

They've already spoken two monologues today, but now they will write a monologue for a character. The character can be one they developed from any of the *Creating Character* lessons or be wholly original. However, only characters with a completed *The Eight W's of Character Development* worksheet (worksheet D) should be considered so that there's biographical information already in place.

Sample Monologues

Without too much preamble, tell students that you are about to read three monologues and after each one there will be questions.

> **Monologue A**
>
> WOMAN
> This is mad crazy. Look at all this money. This is going to take care of everything. I can't believe it. Oh, well, I better believe it. Looks like this is my lucky day.

Ask students what they learned about the character or situation from this monologue. They will most likely suggest that the woman is young because of the use of "mad crazy" and they may suggest that she won the lottery. Ask them if they know the latter for a fact. Generally speaking, they may guess about the situation, but there are not many concrete facts offered in Monologue A. All we really know is that a woman now has some money and that she may be young.

Next read the second monologue.

> **Monologue B**
>
> CARRIE ANN
>
> (*Looking at something in her hands*) Cherries. Cherries. Cherries. Cherries. Ohmygod. Cherries-Cherries-Cherries-Cherries. *(pauses for a moment and takes it all in)* Can this be what I think it is? Can this be real? I happen to tell a random stranger about my problems and like a guardian angel he swoops down to save the day. Oh, um, maybe I should get him some coffee. Do guardian angels even drink coffee? My God. Lucille is going to be fine. This kind of money is going to make everything fine. I need to call Dr. Angelo and schedule us in like now. And when Frank gets in – whenever he bothers to roll out of bed – I'm going to walk into his office, look him straight in the eye and tell him, "you can take this job and shove it 'cause I quit!" And if Lucille gets better – *when* – *when* Lucille gets better, I'll take her to Florida and enroll her in one of those fancy schools and we'll go to Disney World everyday. This man – this-this-this this angel – has no idea that today he saved not one life, but two. Yeah, maybe I should get him some coffee. He can have all the coffee he wants.

Ask the following questions after the second monologue:

- What's this woman's job?
- How do they know that?
- Where does the scene take place?
- What does she mean by "Cherries. Cherries. Cherries. Cherries"?
- Who is the man she refers to?
- Why does she say he's her guardian angel?
- What does the man give her?
- Why does he give her something?
- Who is Lucille?
- What might be wrong with Lucille?
- What's the name of the doctor?
- What's the name of the woman's boss?
- What's the woman's relationship to her job?

After you have thoroughly reviewed the second monologue with the class, reveal that these two monologues are for the same exact character in the same exact situation. In Monologue A, however, we learn only a little information whereas in Monologue B we are given so much more.

Show the pictures of House A and House B (worksheets E and F) introduced in the *Creating Character I* lesson and point out that Monologue A is like the version of the sketched house while Monologue B is like the version of the detailed house.

Which version do students think audiences would appreciate hearing more?

Lastly, read the third monologue.

> **Monologue C**
>
> CARRIE ANN, the WAITRESS
>
> Wow! I was telling this middle-aged customer with a moustache all about the fact that my daughter needs an operation and then when I gave him the bill, he told me that he had enough money to pay for the cheddar cheese omelet, hash browns and orange juice he ordered, but, unfortunately, he didn't have enough to give me a tip because he only had ten dollars on him and the bill was $9.96, so he offered me a scratch-off lottery ticket instead. I was kind of bummed. I really need my tips because Frank, my boss, pays me and the other waiters so terribly. I figured I'd win maybe five dollars at the most or nothing at the worst. But oh, well, at least he was a nice customer. Then I scratched the ticket off and I won the whole jackpot. My twelve-year-old daughter, Lucille, is now going to be able to have that surgery she needs on her kidney and everything is going to be okay!

Like the second monologue (B), the third monologue (C) offers a lot of details, but to some extent, it offers too many. Audiences like to feel smart in figuring some stuff out on their own, so try not to spoon-feed every detail to them.

Outer versus Inner

Before they start writing, review with the class the difference between outer and inner monologues. Take a moment to go over the differences, perhaps providing a brief example.

> **Outer Monologue**: When the character speaks directly to somebody and that other person is aware of being spoken to.
>
> **Inner Monologue**: When the character speaks his/her thoughts out loud either to the audience or themself.

Monologue Focus

While it might be interesting to have a character share a random monologue about the time he slipped on a banana or the time he took a trip to New Jersey, remind students to keep their monologue connected to the character's journey. Carrie Ann's second monologue is about the moment she realizes she'll be able to afford her daughter's operation. A monologue about how she organizes her sock drawer just isn't relevant. Keep monologues focused. Other words of advice to share with your students:

- Monologues often happen at heightened and impassioned moments or an important moment during the play or your character's life.

- There should be a convincing reason why the character giving an outer monologue does not get interrupted by the person they are speaking to. Again, passion or anger or somebody who really needs to speak from the heart and be heard are useful here.

- Monologues should reveal something about the character.
- Keep your monologue present and active, so it's not a character just telling us about a story they remember.

Activity: Write and Share Monologue

The Writing

Give students a moment to review the character that they have created and the corresponding *Eight W's* worksheet.

Have students single out a critical moment when their character has something important to say.

Examples: The moment when...

- Dr. Angelo tells a stunned Carrie Ann that her daughter needs an operation. (outer monologue)
- Lucille is in the hospital again and Carrie Ann tells herself that she will stop at nothing to make this a better world for her daughter. (inner monologue)
- Carrie Ann, filled with anger, walks into Frank's office to give him a piece of her mind and to quit her job. (outer monologue)

Before they write their monologue, have students answer the following three questions at the top of their page:

Question 1: What moment are you writing from your play?

Question 2: Why is this a moment for a monologue?

Question 3: Is this an inner or an outer monologue? If outer, who is your character speaking to?

Monologue lengths vary, but if students are writing by hand, I tell them to aim for three quarters of a page single-spaced.

Lastly, remind them to incorporate passion and details, and to use language that is specific to their character.

Give students 7-10 minutes to write and revise.

The Sharing

Have students partner with a neighbor. Student A briefly provides context and pertinent backstory, then reads their monologue to Student B. After A finishes, B comments, mentions details that stood out and asks questions if anything was unclear. Then it is B's turn.

While this is going on, walk around the room and skim a few monologues that aren't currently being read aloud to look for potential examples to share with the rest of the class.

Afterwards, ask for volunteers to share their monologue with everybody. If you don't get any volunteers, read a few monologues that stood out to you while you walked around. But usually, there are volunteers. Before they read, have them provide any pertinent details that are useful for the audience to know.

Reflection: Kings speak differently than giants. And giants speak differently than you. Despite the differences, we can always imagine what it would be like (and sound like) to be somebody we are not. Just as a city kid probably wouldn't say, "y'all come back now, ya hear" or a grandmother wouldn't say, "what's poppin', yo?" the words we give our characters to speak should be true to that character. And the moment they speak a monologue should be a moment where they have something important to express.

Follow-Up: No piece of art is necessarily perfect the first time through. Have students revise their monologue with a minimum of three changes or additions. At the bottom of the page, ask them to write down the reason why they made each change. Additionally, have them list what happens immediately before and after the monologue.

8   Track Work

By now, you've built a solid playwriting foundation for your students, covering a number of key topics such as character; wants; conflict; beginning, middle and end; plot diagrams; dialogue and monologue. Now it is time to pick the playwriting track that works for you and your class. (For an overview on track differences, see page 3.) To review…

Track I

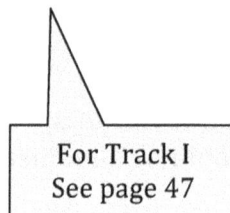

For students writing a play on their own, their next steps are:

- Develop a story sketch and a plot diagram
- Write Section I: The Beginning (2-4 pages)
- Write Section II: The Middle (6-8 pages)
- Write Section III: The End (1-3 pages)

Track II

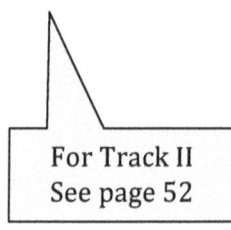

For students writing plays in small groups (ideally groups of 4), their next steps are:

- Create and develop a protagonist and an antagonist
- Generate a story sketch and a plot diagram
- Divide the story, decide who does what, then write individual sections (each student writes 2-3 pages of the play)
- Put it all together and work on transitions

Track III

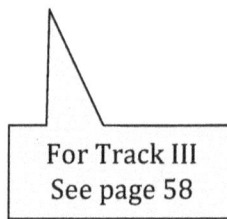

For writing a single play with the entire class, the next steps are:

- Brainstorm play possibilities and main characters
- Come up with supporting roles, story sketch and plot diagram
- Break down scenes and develop characters
- Co-write scenes (each group writes 2-3 pages)
- Put it all together

I recommend reading through all three tracks regardless of the one you select to follow. You may find additional useful activities in the two other methods. Also, be sure to allow time for revision work after drafts are completed. For more on revisions, see page 67.

9   Track I: Individual Playwright Plays

This track can be the most demanding, but it can also be the most fulfilling as each student will write an entire play on their own. Because the majority of the work from now on will be comprised of the actual writing of the plays as well as class feedback, I will not provide a new session for each section, but rather give full instructions here. It is up to you to schedule it into your class' timetable. I recommend a minimum of four additional sessions for this track, which does not include the *Review, Revision and Rubric* session.

Now that you've covered the previous lessons, to summarize, your students have:

- Created and developed their own character
- Written a monologue for said character during a critical moment
- Come up with three possible scenes for their character's play

...which means that much of the ground work for their play is complete.

To outline the remaining steps, students will:

1. Develop a story sketch and plot diagram
2. Write Section I: The Beginning (2-4 pages)
3. Write Section II: The Middle (6-8 pages)
4. Write Section III: The End (1-3 pages)

After each of these four steps, allocate time for peer or class review. You can choose to have students write, share and review their work all in class or you can assign scene writing as homework then share and review during class time. How you structure this depends on how much time you have for the unit. Some teachers see their students everyday, while others only once a week. The structure depends on your specific circumstances.

After students complete a draft of their play, proceed to the *Review, Revision and Rubric* session on page 67. You can give them the rubric ahead of time as a guide.

Step One: Develop a Story Sketch and a Plot Diagram

Have students review the character whose story they will be telling. If they've decided to write about a different character than the one they originally created, they should complete another *The Eight W's of Character Development* worksheet (worksheet D). The more they know about their character at the outset, the easier it is to begin writing the play.

Review the *Plot Diagram* (worksheet C) that you introduced in the *Plot Sequencing* session. Students worked on this in small groups using a fairy tale as the central plot. Now on their own, it's their turn to create a plot diagram and story sketch for their specific character.

Hand out the *Play Framework* (worksheet G) and review any vocabulary questions. As a class, create a story sketch for a character together. This can either be based on a character that is new or one that you've used previously in class. For example:

Sample Story Sketch	
Exposition and Inciting Incident	
Main Character's Name:	Arianna Morales
Main Character's Want:	To be reunited with her family
Inciting Incident:	She accidentally gets separated from her parents while on vacation in Rome.
Main Conflict/Problem:	She scared, lost and doesn't speak Italian.
Rising Actions	
Complication #1:	Instead of staying put like her parents told her to, she goes looking for them and gets herself even more lost.
Complication #2:	Her phone dies because she didn't charge it like her parents reminded her to and now texting and her translation app are no longer available.
Complication #3:	Without a map or the language, she tries to find her way to the American Embassy before it closes at 5pm. It's already 4:15pm.
Climax and Afterwards	
Climax Question:	Will she make it to the embassy in time?
Climax Answer:	She gets there at 4:55pm only to discover that it is closed because it's the 4th of July.
Falling Action:	For the first time in the day, she breaks down crying on the embassy steps just as her mom and dad (who have been looking for her) arrive.
Denouement:	She hugs them and promises to never leave their side again and to always charge her cell phone whenever they leave home or hotel.

Overcoming Plot Hurdles

In the above example, other then Arianna's parents, there aren't any other characters mentioned for Arianna to interact with. And any who appeared would most likely speak Italian. This would be a hurdle for me if I were actually writing the play. Because plays happen in dialogue, I would need to find a way to have Arianna actively communicate with other people. I might tweak it by having her run into an Italian fruit seller who speaks very basic English or maybe I'd give Arianna a sibling so that the two of them are lost together. This way, dialogue is bound to happen.

After completing a story sketch as a class, have students work individually to create one for their own story. On the right side of the *Play Framework* worksheet is a blank plot diagram. Once they've completed the story sketch on the left, they should tentatively plot the story out on the diagram.

This doesn't mean that things can't change. Sometimes when I write, a character does not necessarily go where I want her to go. And that's okay. In fact it's rather exciting to be surprised by one's characters. The map and sketch provide a framework and an option to either follow or veer from. If a student ever is stuck or needs help, referring to this completed document can get them back on track.

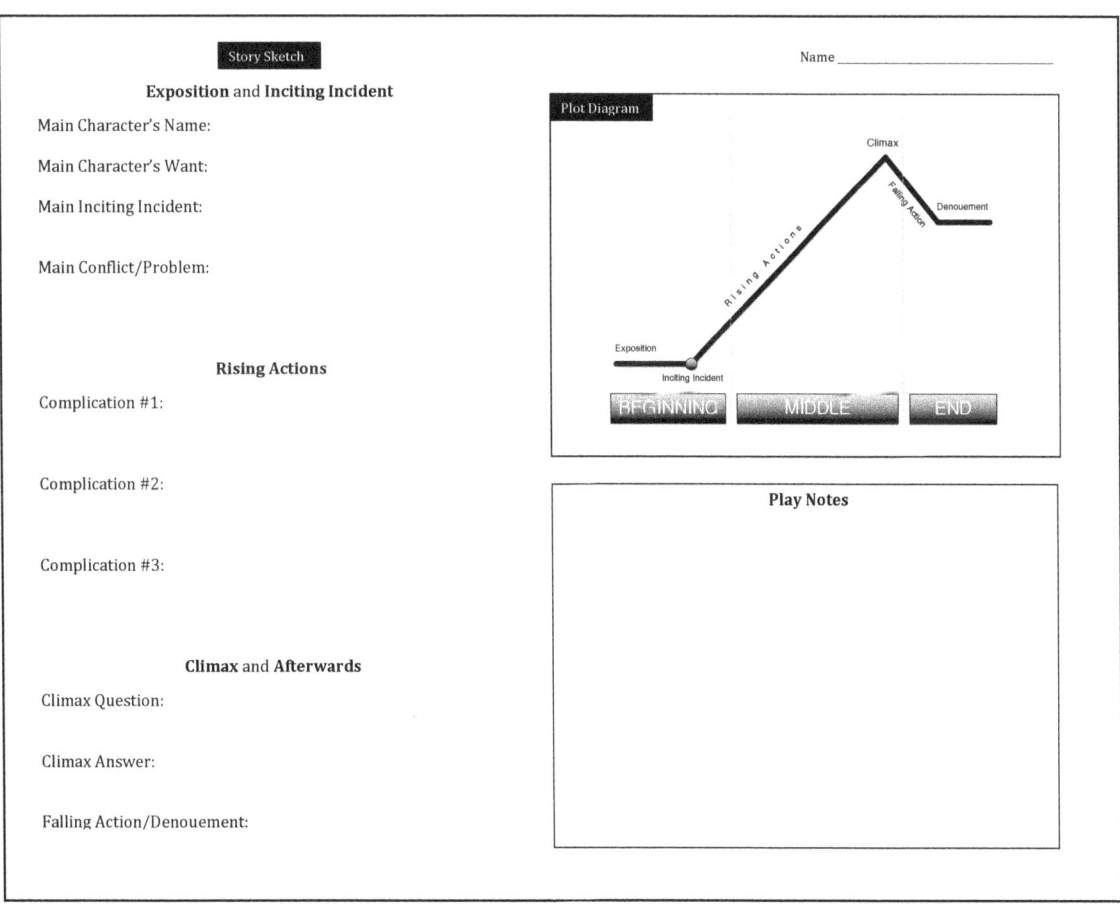

After students complete the worksheet, have them pair up and share with their partner. Alternatively, if you have a small group, students can present to the class. Afterwards, instruct students to provide constructive feedback and pose any pertinent questions the playwright might want to take into consideration. Is this an original idea? Do the characters have potential to intrigue and delight? Is the protagonist likeable? The bottom right hand corner is for playwright notes.

Now comes the actual writing.

Step Two: Write Section I: The Beginning

The writing process is more manageable if you approach each writing section separately. For *Section I* have students write the first scene or moment of their play. This beginning section should include:

- Exposition
- Inciting Incident

This section should be approximately 2-4 pages long. If your students are typing their scripts, I recommend that you review *Script Formatting* (worksheet H) to encourage them to format their plays as they write.

In class, have students pair up to share and comment on each other's opening scene. Is the possibility of an exciting story being set up? Are characters and relationships clear? Is language specific to character? Is the inciting incident strong enough to make an audience interested in wanting to know what happens next?

For homework, they should revise their opening section and then move on to the second section.

Step Three: Write Section II: The Middle

The second section is the bulk of the play and where the story's main development occurs. This middle section should include the following rising actions and climax:

- Complication #1
- Complication #2
- Complication #3
- Climax

This section should be approximately 6-8 pages long. Because there's a double space between each character's block of text, it is amazing how quickly one reaches the end of a page. Although 6-8 pages may sound like a lot to your students, in reality, it's not. Remind them to pace themselves and aim to develop things organically. Also, encourage them to incorporate the character monologue they've already written.

In class, they should again share and review with a partner. Do scenes have a natural, organic build? Do things make sense? Is the playwright building in suspense so that the reader is eager to find out what happens next? Does the climax feel like the high point of the play? Is there sufficient reason for the reader to care about the story and its outcome?

If you have enough time, I recommend spending two days on this section as opposed to one.

For homework, have students revise their middle section based on class notes.

Step Four: Write Section III: The End

Students have reached the apex of the play, so in theory, the third section should be smooth going as it's easier to roll down the plot diagram mountain then it is to climb up it. The key is to set everything up adequately beforehand. I recommend keeping this section concise at around 1-3 pages and it should contain:

- Falling Action
- Denouement

Once completed, they should share and review with their partner. Have all loose ends been tied up? Did the protagonist go on a journey and change in any way by the end of the piece? Is there a clear beginning, middle and end? Were there any enjoyable twists or surprises in the story?

For homework, have students revise their last section based on class notes. In addition to a clear story arc and a gratifying character journey, are there any last bells and whistles to add? Are they satisfied with the story that they have told? Anything else they would add or change?

Now that each student has a completed draft of their play, take a look at the *Review, Revision and Rubric* session on page 67. Although students have made edits and improvements along the way, peer and self-evaluation are useful tools for revising.

Reflection: Congratulations! Each one of your students has just completed an entire one-act play. Although they wrote a short one-page script in an earlier unit, they now have a fleshed-out piece of work just waiting to be performed by actors and seen on a stage. Both you and your students should be very proud of this accomplishment.

Follow-Up: This depends on your class size. If you have a small class, performing all plays aloud is feasible. If you have thirty students, however, that may be too many plays to present. A few teachers I work with have students vote as a class and the top four or five selected plays get performed. There seems to be no hard feelings as those students not selected still get to act and be involved in other ways. But this is all up to you. Before proceeding to play performance, check out the *Performance Crash Course* session on page 81.

10 Track II: Small Group Plays

Communication and collaboration are key to this playwriting track. When students are writing plays in small groups, it is one hundred percent a team effort and as such it is essential for them to be on the same page about all aspects of the play. If you are able to rearrange your classroom, a cluster desk set-up works really well for this writing method. I recommend an additional four sessions for this playwriting track.

As you've completed the playwriting foundation work from previous sessions, at this point your students have:

- Produced and developed their own character
- Plot sequenced a story as a small group
- Generated play ideas from the *"Wouldn't It be Amazing…"* follow-up activity

Instead of having students attempt to base their group play on work they did individually in previous sessions (all useful groundwork) I recommend that groups start fresh as a team.

Therefore the next steps for each group are:

1. Create and develop a protagonist and an antagonist
2. Generate a story sketch and a plot diagram
3. Divide the story, decide who does what, then write individual sections
4. Put it all together and work on transitions

Step One: Create and Develop a Protagonist and an Antagonist

You can use any creating character method for small group plays. My advice is to set-up a clear conflict with a likeable protagonist and a strong antagonist. So if you decide to create characters from a photo, I would give groups not one, but two pictures.

Example: I once gave a group of four students a picture of an African American man in a white tuxedo and a picture of an older Asian woman sitting at a piano. They came up with a storyline where the man (the pictured protagonist) and a woman were in love and wanted to get married, but the woman's mother (the pictured antagonist) was old world and old school and she believed in arranged marriages and wanted her daughter to marry a Japanese man.

No matter which character creation method you choose, have groups complete *The Eight W's of Character Development* (worksheet D) for both characters. Emphasize the importance of details and remind groups that an antagonist does not have to be bad or evil, they just has to be in opposition to the protagonist's wants.

After the two characters are developed, give each group a few minutes to present the protagonist and antagonist to the rest of the class. This enables input from their peers, plus you can provide your own feedback. Pay particular attention to the protagonist's want. Is it a meaty enough subject to base a play on? Does it warrant the possibility of high stakes and an exciting climax? Does the antagonist have strong enough reasons for opposing the protagonist?

Give groups some time to revise and add details to their two character sketches based on the class' feedback and/or questions.

Step Two: Generate a Story Sketch and a Plot Diagram

Now that their two main characters are created, the next step for each group is to generate a rough sketch of the storyline, then plot it on a diagram.

Hand out the *Play Framework* (worksheet G) and review any vocabulary questions.

To familiarize students with this new worksheet, create a story sketch as a class. You can either base it on a new idea or on a character example you've used previously. I provide a sample story sketch example on page 48.

Then have each group develop a story sketch for their prospective play with one student elected as the group scribe to fill in the worksheet. Instruct them to come up with two additional characters to fit into the play. They need not be large roles, but what that does is give each student in the group a part to perform when the play is read out loud. In terms of rising action, remind students that as with the *Brother, Can You Spare a Dime?* activity on page 16, complications should be organic and sequential. Meaning don't jump from complication A to C then back to B, instead each complication should top the last one.

After they have a story sketched out, provide them with markers and a sizeable sheet of butcher paper so they can make a large-scale plot diagram of their play. Have them draw the diagram and then fill it in with the various steps of their story including:

| **Exposition** | **Three Rising Actions** | **Falling Action** |
| **Inciting Incident** | **Climax** | **Denouement** |

If there's time at the end of the session, have each group present their plot diagram to the rest of the class (if there is not, start with presentations next time). Give them a few minutes to prepare and tell them that each student is responsible for a part of their group's presentation.

Have the class give feedback on each group's plot diagram. Are they missing any steps in the rising actions? Does the climax feel like the high point? Is there potential drama to the whole story? (Even comedic stories can and should have a sense of the dramatic.) Are the complications actual complications?

> **Example**: "Rodney and Eric meet to discuss the problem" is not a complication. However, "Rodney threatens to close the homeless shelter unless Eric leaves town" is.

For homework, have group members collaborate on revising and fleshing out their plot diagrams based on notes you and others have given them.

Step Three: Divide, Decide and Write

If you didn't have time in the last class session for groups to share their plot diagram presentation, do so now. Otherwise have groups present any clarifications or revisions they made to their diagrams.

To keep groups on the same page with not only their play arc, but also the genre and style of their play, start Step Three with a warm-up writing activity.

First Line, Last Line

Ask each group to find a critical moment in their plot where one of their characters is so impassioned that they would feel the need to give a monologue. Once that moment is chosen, have the group collectively agree on a first line of the monologue and a last line of the monologue, then have them present both sentences to the class. Make sure that the first and last lines are far enough apart that there is room for potential growth in the monologue.

Another option is to have groups present their critical moment and let the class collectively suggest first and last lines for each group's monologue. You would be able to oversee and ensure that the line pairings enable potential growth within the monologue.

Here are two examples:

Moment:	The moment when Anthony confronts Mrs. Kimura about wanting to marry her daughter.
First Line:	*You think Kioko wants to disappoint you?*
Last Line:	*You may not approve of me, Mrs. Kimura-san, but Kioko and I are in love and we will be getting married.*

> **Moment:** When Eric responds to Rodney's threat to close the homeless shelter.
>
> **First Line:** *You are so blowing things out of proportion, Rodney.*
>
> **Last Line:** *I will leave because I care about these people and I want them to have a safe haven, but you're not right, Rod, you're not right.*

Remind students that although there is a beginning, middle and end to everything, things ought to grow and go somewhere. A monologue that remains the same throughout is flat. Challenge them to incorporate nuance and detail.

Once first and last lines of each group are decided, give students 7-10 minutes to write their monologue. The monologue should be about three-quarters of a page.

After the allotted time, each group should have four monologues with the same first and last lines. Have each student read their monologue out loud to the others in their group. Have them keep track of where there were similarities and differences, and also note or circle any lines they thought were particularly moving or enlightening.

This is also a good time for groups to check their monologues for tone. If three monologues are quite impassioned and dramatic while the fourth is flippant and funny, that one student is likely writing and seeing the character very differently. This is not to say that a character in different moments can't be different things. On the contrary, it's good to be multi-faceted human beings (as we actually all are), but checking the tone ensures that group members have a similar understanding of a specific moment.

Divide and Decide

Give each group a set of eight index cards. On one side of each index card have them write:

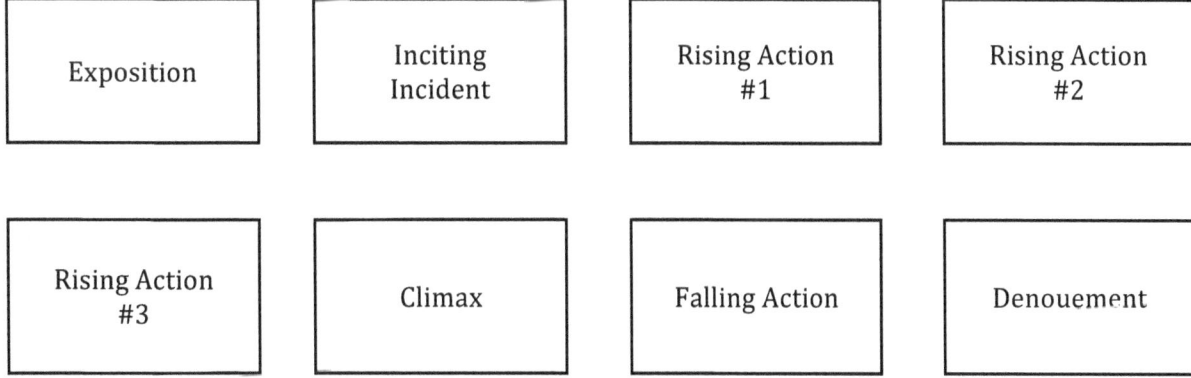

On the back side have them write the specific moment in their play that coincides with the word on the front of the card.

Example: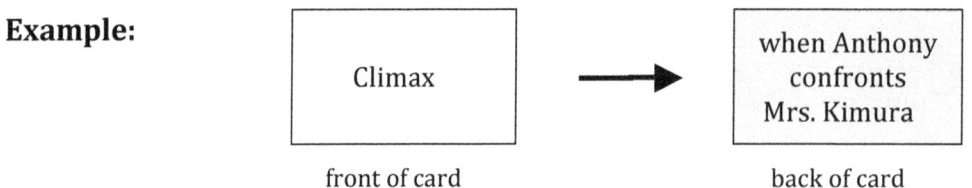

front of card   back of card

Have the students shuffle the cards and pick two each. As a group, it is their task to share the story with each other in its proper sequence. Whoever has "Exposition" begins the story, followed by the person who has "Inciting Incident", then the three "Rising Actions", then "Climax", "Falling Action", and "Denouement" in order.

The objective of this activity is for the entire group to be familiar and comfortable with all aspects of their story and for them all to be on the same page in terms of the overall arc. They are free to add any relevant or interesting details that might occur in their particular scene, which may then be used again in other scenes.

Additionally, they should focus on fluid transitions from one moment to the next. Tell them to think of it like running a relay race. The first runner must be sure that the second runner has the baton securely in hand before letting go. The passing of the baton is crucial.

If there is time, I recommend reshuffling the cards and doing this activity again.

Now that groups really know their story, it's time to decide who writes which moment. Each student is responsible for two sequential moments.

    Student A: Exposition and Inciting Incident
    Student B: Rising Actions #1 and #2
    Student C: Rising Actions #3 and Climax
    Student D: Falling Action and Denouement

And Write

Although 2-3 pages is a sufficient length for each student to write, I recommend that Students B and C write at least three pages each since there is more to develop in their sections. Student C should also be given the four monologues written as part of the *First Line, Last Line* activity to incorporate into the climax as they see fit. If the monologues were written for a different moment in the play, Student C can pass the monologues to the student responsible for that particular moment.

If there is still time left in class, I suggest students start writing. If not, have them work on their scenes as homework. Otherwise, have students write during the next class.

If you want your students to type their scripts, I recommend sharing the *Script Formatting* (worksheet H) with them.

Step Four: Put It All Together and Work on Transitions

Ideally, there are four copies of each student's writing: three to share with the rest of the writing team and one copy for you – plus their original.

In their small groups, students should share their drafted scenes out loud and in order. Have individuals take notes on things that don't make sense or moments that don't transition well into the next.

Examples:
- In scene 1, Eric has two kids, but in scene 3 he has only one kid.
- The student responsible for Rising Actions #1 and #2 has also included Rising Action #3 in his scene.
- Inciting Incident isn't a big enough jolt to get the story going.

After their first read through together, they should discuss each other's notes and tentatively troubleshoot on how to solve any inconsistencies.

For more detailed notes, have each student now read the scene that directly precedes theirs and give specific notes to that particular student. So that:

- Student B reads and comments on Student A's writing
- Student C reads and comments on Student B's writing
- Student D reads and comments on Student C's writing
- Student A reads and comments on Student D's writing

This also gives you time to peruse their draft to make any overall notes you'd like them to work on. See page 67 for more on *Review, Revision and Rubric*.

For homework, have each student revise their section based on group (and your) notes. Also have them come up with four possible titles for their play.

Reflection: Congratulations! Your students have collaborated on writing a group play. They collectively created characters and plot, and were individually responsible for writing parts of the script. The biggest feat was working as a team to accomplish it all. Well done! Next step (after revision work) is to share the plays with the rest of the class.

Follow-Up: For a class of 20-28 students, there will be only 5-7 plays to read out loud which is very doable. Before proceeding to play performance, check out the *Performance Crash Course* session on page 81.

11   Track III: Entire Class Plays

Now here's where things get interesting. Whereas individual plays are a solitary effort and small group plays are akin to a team relay race, the entire class play is not dissimilar from spinning plates all at once. From an outside perspective, it may look difficult – and certainly impressive – but if you know what you are doing and/or follow these steps, a class of 25-30 students can quite quickly and effectively make a worthwhile piece of theater. I suggest an additional 4-6 sessions for this track.

As with the other two tracks, I recommend that you do the groundwork in the earlier sessions. That way, by this point, your students will already be familiar with:

- What a play is
- Creating and developing a character
- Writing monologues, dialogues and stage directions
- Structuring plots from beginning to middle to end

Once you have selected a theme or topic, the next step as a class includes:

1. Brainstorm play possibilities and main characters
2. Come up with supporting roles, story sketch and plot diagram
3. Break down scenes and develop characters
4. Co-write scenes
5. Put it all together

A Word on Choosing Topics

I cannot think of a single educational topic that wouldn't benefit from further exploration in a theatrical way. If there is something you'd like your students to consider in greater detail while maintaining a literary link, it can be done.

I have had students write plays based on:
- an art exhibit of Hindu god sculptures and the Chola Dynasty
- Shakespeare's Marcus Brutus being put on trial for the death of Caesar
- an exploration of ancient Egyptian life and culture
- radio plays which we then recorded complete with sound effects and music

Art, literature, history, and media were the jumping off points for the examples above, but they could have just as easily been math, science or agriculture. What is important is creating believable characters who respond truthfully to the circumstance of any given moment. So have fun picking your topic and make it something you too would like to explore.

To show how I approached one of my playwriting units under this track, I'll walk you through the specific steps I took with three separate 6th grade classes.

Step One: Brainstorm Play Possibilities and Main Characters

Step One can take anywhere from 1-3 days depending on how in-depth you want to go with research. If it is a topic that students are already studying, you won't need much time to introduce it, but if it is something new to them, be sure to factor in a bit more time for adequate preparation.

After you have selected your area of interest for a play, the first thing to do is get your students familiar with the time and the world of the piece and the possible characters who would live in that world.

In teaching playwriting using ancient Egypt as the focus, I had students:

- Read thought-provoking facts about pharaohs that I'd collected and distributed
- Write pharaoh monologues and compose dialogues between gods
- Brainstorm possible professions during our given time period (government official, scribe, soldier, merchant, artisan, performer, farmer, tomb builder, slave)
- Discuss and discover the kernel of an idea we wanted to explore based on the facts that interested them most

The three classes I worked with separately chose the following as their focus:

Class One	was interested in exploring what happens when an Egyptian's ka (spirit/soul) is trapped and cannot move on to the afterlife.
Class Two	was intrigued by the fact that in some royal families, siblings married one another to keep bloodlines 'pure'.
Class Three	wanted to concentrate on the different class system in ancient Egypt and the individual's role within it.

The corresponding main characters we brainstormed were:

Class One	a brother and sister lost in a sandstorm
Class Two	the daughter of a pharaoh
Class Three	a baker and a farmer

For homework, students were tasked with finding an interesting fact online that could be useful to our initial play idea.

Step Two: Supporting Roles, Story Sketch and Plot Diagram

At this point you should have the main idea that you would like to explore in your class play. If you are not using a curriculum tie-in as a springboard, you could easily use one of the ideas from the "*Wouldn't It Be Amazing If...*" activity (page 24). For example, "wouldn't it be amazing if kids lived on Mars" could become the basis of a play about how kids colonize and survive on the red planet. What troubles would they face? Why are they there? Who would the main characters be? The idea is certainly timely and offers a lot to explore.

After sharing the homework assignment out loud in pairs, move on to turning our ideas into stories.

Ideas → Stories + Characters

An idea is just that – the beginning of a thought or suggestion. In Step Two, you and your class will need to hone your idea so that there is a specific and concrete story behind it as well as clear ancillary characters to populate the world. Once you have your main characters and their clear wants established, the characters almost start writing their stories themselves.

> **Example**: In the "royal bloodline" class, the main character is the pharaoh's daughter. Her want is to make her own choices in life and *not* be forced into marrying her brother. Obviously her dad is going to be very opposed to her wishes and fulfill the antagonist role.

As a group, start coming up with plot ideas and a possible character list. For a class of around 25 students, I recommend a play with 6 or 7 characters.

With short plays, I don't always recommend writing larger cast pieces with a variety of smaller roles, however, when 25 students are involved in the creation process of a single play, it is important to make opportunities for smaller group work – which more characters allows for.

The story and characters my three classes came up with were:

Class One	
Story:	A brother and sister accidentally open a secret door to a tomb, which helps lift the curse that a god placed on three ghosts whose spirits have been locked up for thousands of years.
Characters:	Brother, sister, ghost guard, ghost pyramid builder, ghost embalmer, the goddess

Class Two	
Story:	To keep royal bloodlines pure, the pharaoh wants his daughter to marry her brother, but she wants to be free to make her own decisions in life.
Characters:	The pharaoh, his wife, their son, their daughter, daughter's beloved, daughter's maid (and confidant), a disgruntled ex-employee of the pharaoh

Class Three	
Story:	A farmer and a baker sick of their current life, decide things would be easier if they were soldiers, but when the pharaoh sends them to war, it's their wives who come to the rescue.
Characters:	Farmer, farmer's wife, baker, baker's wife, a soldier, a general, the pharaoh

To further flesh out your story, answer the story sketch questions on the *Play Framework* (worksheet G) as a class. In individual and small group plays I champion the sole protagonist, but with larger class plays, I usually divide this role and have a duo of co-protagonists. This way there's more to go around (e.g., siblings in Class One and farmer and baker in Class Three).

Plot Diagrams

With the story sketch now in place, it's time to move on to a group plot diagram. On the board, draw a large-scale plot diagram. Then as a class, fill it all in. The more familiarity students have with the storyline and the more they are all on the same page, the easier it will be for them to write. Below is a rough guide for the "royal bloodline" plot diagram.

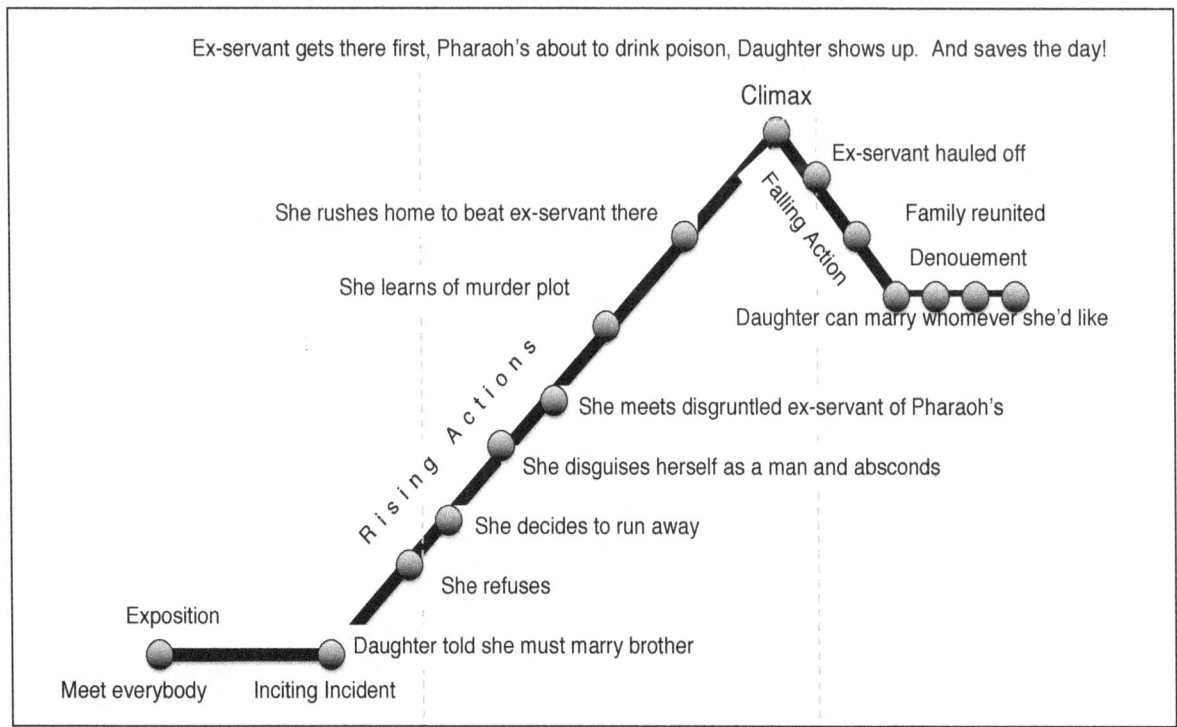

By the end of Step Two, your class should have drawn up a rough plot and chosen all the characters.

Step Three: Scene Breakdown and Character Development

Story → Scenes

Organization is of the essence in large class projects. While a plot diagram and a discussion would be sufficient for a playwriting collaboration in a small group, it is better to be much more definitive with this track. To that extent, the next step is to sketch out the scene framework. With a larger class, I aim for around 7-9 scenes. This enables adequate story development time as well as smaller group writing work. Here's the scene breakdown that we came up with as a class for the "royal bloodline" plot:

Royal Bloodline Scene Breakdown

Scene 1: Meet **Pharaoh Abubakar** and his wife, **Salihah**. Pharaoh says it's high time their daughter got married... to their son.

Scene 2: Meet **Dalila**, the pharaoh's daughter, and her boyfriend, **Zuberi**, who proposes to her and she says yes.

Scene 3: Pharaoh and wife tell Dalila that she is to be wed to her younger brother, **Gyasi**, tomorrow. She says she will not because she wants to marry Zuberi. Innocent Gyasi enters while others storm off.

Scene 4: Dalila decides to run away. She tells her maid and confidant, **Olabisi**, who at first is against the plan, but then decides to help by giving Dalila some men's clothing to dress up in for her escape.

Scene 5: Pharaoh and wife cannot find their daughter and so they question Olabisi, who manages to keep the secret safe.

Scene 6: A disguised Dalila accidentally bumps into a stranger, **Jabari**, as she is running away. They commiserate because neither of them likes the pharaoh, but Jabari's hatred of Abubakar seems dangerous.

Scene 7: Dalila's fiancé, Zuberi, and her brother Gyasi have the "I'm going to marry her", "No, I'm going to marry her" scene.

Scene 8: Back on the road, Jabari tells Dalila that he is going to poison the pharaoh. Jabari leaves. While Dalila still wants to run away, now she's scared for her father's life and doesn't know what to do.

Scene 9: Jabari comes to the palace with a special chocolate drink he made for the pharaoh. Olabisi lets him in. Pharaoh, wife and son appear. Abubakar is about to drink the concoction when Dalila enters and saves the day. Jabari is hauled off by Olabisi. The pharaoh is grateful to Dalila for saving his life. Both he and his wife express remorse over the disagreement with their daughter and say they just want her to be happy. And if marrying Zuberi will make her happy, then so be it. She shall be allowed to make her own choices and get married to whomever she'd like.

Character Representatives

Character work is something your students will have already done individually, but now it will be a team effort.

Divide the class up into as many groups as you have characters in your play. In my example, there were seven characters in a class of 25. As I noticed that the daughter is in the bulk of the scenes, I decided to make her group larger. Hence, I had one group of five, two groups of four and four groups of three.

Each one of the individuals in these groups is considered a representative for their team's character (i.e., a group of five character reps for the daughter, a group of four character reps for the pharaoh, etc.). Right now, character reps are working together to develop a character, but in Step Four they won't be, which is why it is important to empower and encourage every student to know as much about their character as possible and to collaborate with their co-character reps on the character's development.

Each group is in charge of one character and the development of that character. Character reps should complete an *Eight W's of Character Development* (worksheet D) keeping in mind that their answers, in this case, should ideally relate to the plot they've already created as a class.

I came up with a few follow-up questions to keep them focused on the play:

- Which character does your group have?
- What is the name you've chosen for your character?
- Why have you chosen this name?
- How old is the character?
- What is their job?
- What are three responsibilities that they have?
- In the play, what does he/she want?
- Why does he/she want it?
- What does he/she do to get it?
- Who or what gets in the way?

I gave students a list of around 80 Egyptian names with paired meanings. Reps then selected a name for their character based on name meanings: the Pharaoh is noble, Wife is agreeable, Daughter is gentle, Maid brings joy; etc...

Key Reasons

In the interest of creating *detailed* work, as a class we came up with two additional open-ended key questions for each character rep team. This can either be given as homework or can be done in class. Have all students answer questions individually. That way, instead of just one or two answers per character rep team, there will be a pool of possibilities. Not every answer has to be incorporated into the final play, but having multiple possibilities are useful when reps begin scene writing. This also enables reps to get to know their specific character a bit better.

Here's the list of requests that we came up with:

Character Rep Reason Requests	
Daughter:	2 reasons why she doesn't want to marry her brother.
	2 things she can say to the angry servant to defend the pharaoh.
Pharaoh:	2 reasons why he wants his daughter to marry his son.
	2 things he could say when he confronts the maid.
Wife:	2 things she admires about the pharaoh.
	2 reasons she wants her daughter to marry.
Boyfriend:	2 specific reasons why he loves the daughter.
	2 non-threatening things he can say to the brother.
Maid:	1 detailed idea of how she can help the daughter escape.
	3 lies she might tell the pharaoh to cover up for the daughter's disappearance.
Brother:	2 reasons why he wants to marry who his father says to.
	2 non-threatening things he can say to the boyfriend.
Ex-Servant:	3 reasons why he dislikes the pharaoh so much.
	1 idea of how he plans to poison the pharaoh.

Step Four: Co-write Scenes (in small groups)

Who's Where When

Take a moment to jot down which character is in each scene and make note of how many scenes each character gets. Having easy access to this information is crucial in keeping tabs on which students will be working on which scene.

Who's in What

Scene 1: Pharaoh, Wife
Scene 2: Daughter, Boyfriend
Scene 3: Pharaoh, Wife, Daughter, Brother
Scene 4: Daughter, Maid
Scene 5: Pharaoh, Wife, Maid
Scene 6: Daughter, Ex-Servant
Scene 7: Boyfriend, Brother
Scene 8: Daughter, Ex-Servant
Scene 9: All

Character	Scenes	Total
Pharaoh	1, 3, 5, 9	4 scenes
Wife	1, 3, 5, 9	4 scenes
Daughter	2, 3, 4, 6, 8, 9	6 scenes
Boyfriend	2, 7, 9	3 scenes
Brother	3, 7, 9	3 scenes
Maid	4, 5, 9	3 scenes
Ex-Servant	6, 8, 9	3 scenes

If you find that one character is only in a single scene, you and your class will need to either find a valid reason for them to be involved in another scene or make sure that they are featured greatly in their one scene. (If they are only in one scene, I'd assign fewer character reps to that group.)

Grouping by Scene
Arrange the class in as many areas as you have scenes. The "royal bloodline" play had nine scenes and so we needed nine groupings of desks. Each area should have a sheet of paper with the following information: scene number, characters involved, a brief scene synopsis and then a blank space to fill-in the writers' names.

Scene #:	Scene Two
Characters:	Dalila and Zuberi
Synopsis:	We meet the pharaoh's daughter and her boyfriend who proposes to her and she says yes.
Writers:	_____

This is the point where character reps split from their original team in order to branch out. Either assign or have character reps volunteer which one of their character's scenes they would like to write.

Example: Olabisi, the maid, is in three scenes (4, 5, 9) and she has three character reps (A, B, C) on her team. Her reps split up for the writing portion so that:

- Rep A works on scene 4 (with a daughter rep).
- Rep B works on scene 5 (with a pharaoh rep and a wife rep).
- Rep C works on scene 9 (along with reps from all other characters).

Once the writing groups are established and they have reviewed what they need to cover in their scene, they should begin writing. I recommend a 2-3 page limit for each group. Some scenes may need slightly less, some perhaps more. Decide as per the needs of your project.

Make it clear to students that scenes must have:

- a beginning, middle, and end
- any pertinent stage directions
- the required scene characters
- the required scene plot points

It is important that students only write what needs to happen in their particular scene. For example, in Scene Two Dalila has no idea that the pharaoh is going to force her to marry her brother. She also has no idea that in a later scene she will decide to run away. The main event that needs to happen in Scene Two is that we meet Dalila and her boyfriend for the first time and that he must propose to her by the end of the scene and she must say yes.

Step Five: Putting It Together

Step Five begins with any notes you may have when you read the whole script in order. Are there areas that need further development? Did what was supposed to occur in every scene happen? Does it look like scenes will flow smoothly into one another or do some transitions need to be created?

If you don't have many notes, a small rewriting team can perhaps address this, but if you have enough notes for the entire class, by all means, have them regroup. Take a look at the session on *Review, Revision and Rubric* (page 67) for more ideas on active rewriting questions.

If the groundwork has been properly laid, and character reps are consistent with their team's character, and scene writers know what needs to happen in their scene, then it should all come together quite seamlessly.

Reflection: Spinning plates accomplished – Congratulations! You and your class now have a multi-faceted one-act play. This track is very much an "it takes a village" sort of project, so well done on getting the whole village on the same page.

Follow-Up: The next step is to share the play out loud. You can either cast one actor per character (in which case only a handful of students get the opportunity to perform) or you can choose to have a character be played by a different actor in each scene. If you decide to do the latter, consider a simple costume piece that is consistent with the role that all actors playing the same character can wear (e.g., all pharaohs wear the same headdress, all Dalilas wear a purple shirt, etc.). Before proceeding to acting the play, check out the *Performance Crash Course* session on page 81.

12 Review, Revision, Rubric

Activity: Review

Peer-review and self-review are two methods that can help prepare for revision work. Once a draft is completed, recommend playwrights self-evaluate their script and also read and evaluate the script of at least one other playwright. See the bullet points below to use as a guide. If possible, give playwrights the opportunity to hear some of their work read out loud by other students so the playwright can get a sense of whether their intentions are being achieved.

Before peer-review, open a discussion on what constitutes constructive comments and useful questions. Remind reviewers to be polite, encouraging, positive and specific. Their role is not to "fix" the other person's play or decide what they would do if they were in the playwright's position. They are to reflect on what they've read, and note what works and what still needs some attention.

Self-Review

- What I think about this current draft:
- The thing I like best about my play (and why):
- The area where I feel it needs the most work:
- A question I have about my play that would be useful to get feedback on:
- A specific challenge I still have and how I might address it:
- What I would like audiences to get out of my play:

Peer-Review

- The thing I like best about the play:
- The area where I feel it needs the most work:
- Why I think that specific area needs work:
- A question I have for the playwright for them to think about:
- One specific and useful recommendation I have for the playwright:

> **Sample questions a playwright might have about their own work:**
> - How can I make my ending stronger?
> - Is there something confusing in my play and if so, how can I fix it?
> - What would make my character(s) more believable?
> - Is there a scene missing that would add more conflict or suspense to the plot?
> - What did you find surprising about my play?

Teacher Review

Questions are a useful tool for both the commenting and the creative process. Good questions can activate a playwright's thinking and hopefully open up their mind to possibilities.

Specific inquiries regarding a character's want, obstacle and/or action enables a playwright to focus on honing specific answers and reasons, so that things aren't nebulous or generalized.

"What's the scene about?" will produce less useful answers than "Why does Anya want Billy to come to the party?" The specificity of the second question is more likely to warrant a more thoughtful answer.

Activity: Revision

Tell students to go through their play and address notes that you and their peer reviewer(s) may have had. They also must address their own self-review notes.

If you find that some students are having difficulty with knowing what to do about their notes, you can always troubleshoot with the entire class on general topics such as: deepening character, being more original, lengthening scenes, etc. Conversely, you can have playwrights work in smaller groups to troubleshoot their notes.

Most Significant Changes

A teacher I work with and admire greatly, Mrs. Alison Stahl of Clark Lane Middle School in Waterford, CT, has her 8th grade students each write a play to submit to the Young Playwrights Festival that I run at the Eugene O'Neill Theater Center. Upon completing their final draft, Mrs. Stahl asks her students to list the four "Most Significant Changes" they made to their play. Not only is this useful for the playwright, but it also helps you gauge what they consider significant and how successful those changes were.

Activity: Rubric

Creativity can be difficult to grade, but process, formatting, review and revision are all measureable and assessable. To that extent, I have suggested a rubric for individual plays on the following page. Group plays and entire class plays can follow a similar rubric. With Mrs. Stahl's permission, I have also included her 30-point revision breakdown. If you would prefer to use a proficiency-based system over point-based, I would still recommend incorporating process, formatting, review and revision into your rubric.

Sample Rubric

Process	50 points total
Plot diagram and character worksheet	5 points
Plot diagram revision	5 points
Beginning section (exposition, inciting incident)	10 points
Middle section (rising actions, climax)	15 points
End section (falling action, denouement)	10 points
Completed first draft	5 points

Formatting	10 points total
Proper formatting	5 points
Title page and character description sheet	5 points

Review	10 points total
Self-review	5 points
Peer-review	5 points

Revision				30 points total	
Addressed all areas of note, including difficult areas	Addressed most areas of note, including difficult areas	Addressed more than half of areas of concern	Addressed several areas – most were easy changes	Addressed few areas – all easy changes
(30-27 pts)	(26-24 pts)	(23-21 pts)	(20-18 pts)	(17-0 pts)

13   The Playwright's Checklist

As playwrights are writing and rewriting, here is a list of questions and notes for them to keep in mind.

Ideas

- Is my idea well suited for a play, as opposed to a movie?
- Is my play idea original?
- Have I thought of an interesting title, which is true to the play and would quite possibly make audiences want to know more?
- Is the journey a fulfilling one that audiences would want to watch?
- Are there elements of surprise and suspense in my play?

Character and Dialogue

- Am I sticking to essential characters?

In a short play, it's easier for the audience to take in – and for the playwright to introduce – three characters rather than twelve. If there are unnecessary roles, like a neighbor with one line, can the story be told without them?

- Is it clear who the main character is? And what he/she wants?
- Are my characters fully developed?
- Does my protagonist experience a change by the end of the play?
- Is there a clear reason why the main character's journey must happen now?

Sometimes there isn't a strong enough reason as to why a play even starts. But if it is the day of the big exam, or the day that a boy decides he's had enough and he's going to stand up to his bullies, or the day when the pharaoh decides his daughter must marry; in other words, if the stakes are high enough, a ticking time clock of pressure is embedded and stakes will automatically be raised. So make it an important day in your character's life.

- Does my characters' dialogue sound natural and/or believable?

Structure, Development and Execution

- Is my exposition concise, yet sufficient?

Within a 10-15 page play, there isn't a lot of time to spend on exposition. Introduce the characters and then bam, get on with the journey.

- Does my play have a clear beginning, middle and end?
- Am I sticking to essential shifts in time and place?

It's hard to do epic plays in the ten-minute format. The passage of time is essential to a play like, say, *King Lear,* but that play can run for four hours and has the space to dig deep and explore whereas your play is only 10-15 pages. Additionally, if in your stage directions, you use a lot of "*two years later*" and the next scene is "*five years later*" or "*now they're in Las Vegas,*" followed by "*now they're in Ecuador*", it's harder to tell that story live without those stage directions being read aloud. Challenge yourself to write with some semblance of unity of time and place.

- Are the obstacles in my protagonist's way worthwhile and challenging?
- Is the main conflict strong enough? And are the stakes high enough?
- Does the climax feel like the high point of my play?
- How is the pace and development of my scenes?

If scenes feel too short, how can you develop them so that there's more of an organic build to the storytelling? If scenes are too long, how can you distill to more of what is essential?

- Have I edited my stage directions so that only crucial ones remain?

If something is important, reveal it through dialogue. Stage directions like: *"She looks at the ring on her finger and begins to cry; she knows she doesn't love him anymore, so she decides to leave"* are not easily enacted. More effective would be dialogue that covers the action:

Eva:	I can't do this any more. *Takes off ring.*
Alex:	But we made a promise to each other.
Eva:	It's not a promise I feel like I can fulfill now. I wish you the best, Alex, I wish for you the life I couldn't give you. Good-bye.

- If typed, is the play in a standardized format?

14 Miscellaneous Advice

Advice: Choosing a Title

Just like choosing a character's name, deliberate thought should go into choosing a title. I recommend that students keep an ongoing list of possibilities. Good titles stand out for being original and/or true to the play.

Consider this selection of some of Eugene O'Neill's play titles: *A Moon for the Misbegotten, Mourning Becomes Electra, Desire Under the Elms, Strange Interlude, Long Day's Journey into Night, The Iceman Cometh.* They are evocative and powerful. Your students' titles need not be as poetic, but challenge them to think of at least five alternate titles so that they don't necessarily go with the first thing that pops into their head. Sometimes the first thing that pops into our head is the right title, but it is worthwhile to come up with a few others in order to validate the original thought.

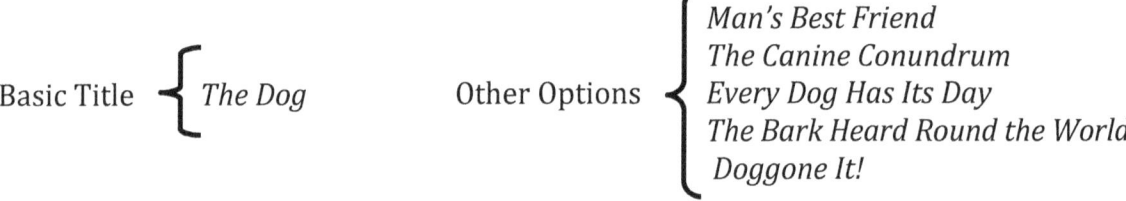

Advice: Punctuation and Grammar

In order to achieve natural sounding dialogue in plays, proper grammar has a tendency to go out the window. Contractions are used more often than not and words such as "yeah", "gimme", and "gonna" are commonplace. Slang and colloquialisms also frequently appear in scripts. All this is not to do a disservice to the rules of the written word, but rather to emulate how we speak in real life.

Whereas correct use of grammar can be somewhat loose in plays, punctuation can be a playwright's greatest ally. Consider the ubiquitous phrase often found on t-shirts: "Let's eat, Grandma" versus "Let's eat Grandma." What a difference a comma can make. Another thing worth reviewing with students is the usefulness of ellipses and em dashes.

Ellipsis is used to indicate trailing off:

>Henry: I thought that if I told her, she'd, well…
>Lidia: She'd what? Come back to us?

The em dash is most often used to denote an interruption or an abrupt break in speech:

>Henry: I thought that probab—
>Lidia: She's not ever coming back, Henry!

A line of dialogue may be interrupted or may trail off; this can be indicated by the ellipsis and em dash, which are essential tools for writing natural sounding dialogue. Additionally, punctuation can be a helpful guide for an actor. Look at the difference between these two sentences:

> I think I love you!
> I...think I love you?

How you punctuate can really affect an actor's interpretation of your characters, so when making revisions check your punctuation so that the play appears how you want it to.

Advice: Know What You're Talking About

There's one school of thought that says, write what you know, while another method says to write what you want to know. Either method is valid, but I must stress, that if you are writing about something you don't know and it is something that your characters should know, then you have your work cut out for you.

I get a lot of play submissions from students eager to show their dramatic writing side. Often times, this is demonstrated by having a character that is sick or dying of a disease (cancer being the most prevalent). Unless the playwright has done their due diligence and researched this topic thoroughly to portray it accurately on stage, it can instead come across a bit reductive.

So while I encourage students to write about things they both know and don't yet know, if they are choosing the latter and want to accurately portray the subject matter, they must do the research.

Advice: Read Writing Out Loud

Another valuable activity is to have students have their work read aloud. This can either be done in pairs or small groups. Being able to hear one's dialogue out loud can provide guidance on whether or not that dialogue is working as intended.

15 Additional Character Activities

This bonus session focuses on broadening and deepening the knowledge of one's character. If ever your students are stuck on how a character would react in a given circumstance or what a character might say in a particular moment, that's when I suggest that students start asking their characters some questions and see if their answers contain anything illuminating or helpful.

Sometimes it's useful to put the play aside and just get to know the character a bit more. The activities below can be done after *The Monologue* session or when students are already involved in playwriting track work. There are a variety of activities on getting to know one's character better and they need not happen all in one session. Feel free to use the activities as warm-up exercises or as a do-now when students enter the classroom.

Activity: A Letter from your Character

Tell your students that they are going to write a letter. The letter is *from* their character and *to* them, the playwright. The letter should begin with:

Dear (Playwright's Name) ,

There's something I need to tell you...

And end with the character signing off.

Give students five minutes to write the letter. Tell them not to censor themselves, but rather put themselves in the place of their character and see what their character has to say. What the character reveals may be surprising, funny, sad, enlightening. It may be useful to the student's play idea or it may not. But in any case, it's a chance for their character to share a little bit more about themselves.

Activity: How your Character Makes Decisions

Your character is at the mall with one hundred dollars to spend. (If your character pre-dates malls or doesn't use dollars as currency, adjust accordingly.) Write a two-page scene between your character and a shop assistant. Start the scene with:

Shop Assistant: Can I help you, sir / ma'am ?

How does your character choose to spend the money? Do they know instantly what they want to buy or are they more measured? Are they a fast decision-maker or slower to process? Do they manage to make a purchase by the end of the scene?

Activity: Routine and Ritual

The alarm goes off. Time for your character to wake up. Write a monologue from your character (in first person) describing what he/she does for the first hour of the waking day. Are they a morning person? A snooze button user? Is it 5 a.m. or almost noon? Do they have a specific routine every morning? Any rituals (e.g., must freshly squeeze oranges before cracking the eggs)?

Activity: 5 by 5 by 5 (Truths, Lies and the Extraordinary)

We are complex human beings with a range of emotions and different sides to us. We are never wholly one thing. And sometimes we are a bag of contradictions. To make your characters more real, give them some range.

Draw three columns down a piece of paper. Label the columns from left to right: 5 Truths, 5 Lies and 5 Extraordinary Facts.

Underneath the first column, write five truths about your character. Underneath the second column, five lies. And underneath the third column, five extraordinary facts about your character.

Example:

5 Truths	5 Lies	5 Extraordinary Facts
- is from Haiti - loves rock-n-roll - has one brother - hates fish - is always late	- is 6 feet tall - doesn't talk fast - can drive a car - scared of heights - is a great cook	- read the entire dictionary in one weekend - was once stuck on an elevator for 6 hours - has a collection of 5000 baseball cards - can name every Ford model ever made - can't sleep without a taco-shaped pillow

You don't have to use all this information. Sharing these fifteen things with an audience might be too much and probably take away from your play. However, similar to the *A House Is Not a Home* activity, it's a good exercise on detail and it's another way for you to get to know your character better.

Activity: One of the Five Senses

Your character is out for a walk one day, when suddenly they see / smell / taste / hear / touch something that brings back a powerful memory to them. Which of the five senses is the one that jolts their memory and what is the memory? Write a monologue from your character's point of view and be sure to include specifics of the memory.

Activity: Character in the Hot Seat

The following questions can be asked all at once or divvied out as desired.

- What did your character have for breakfast this morning?
- What does your character's bedroom look like?
- Describe a special memory of your character.
- What is your character's greatest fear?
- When and where was your character most happy? And why?
- What is your character's life motto?
- What is your character most proud of?
- What does your character like best about him/herself?
- What does your character like least about him/herself?
- What's your character's biggest pet peeve?
- What doesn't your character like people to know about him/her?
- What are three words your character would use to describe him/herself?
- What are three words others would use to describe your character?
- What's your character's relationship like with his/her family?
- What was the most important day or life changing moment of your character's life?

Activity: A Lunch Date

You have agreed to meet your character who has invited you out to lunch.

Option A: Decide who gets there first. Then write a short scene starting from the moment the second person arrives.

Option B: Write about the lunch after the fact as a journal entry. If you choose this method, begin the entry with: *Today I had lunch with (Character Name) at (Restaurant Name)* .

With either option, be sure to include: What does your character order? How does he/she speak to the waiter? Why has he/she chosen this restaurant? What do you talk about while you wait for the food to arrive?

Activity: The Difference a Mood Makes

Select a simple activity that your character does regularly.

Examples: Making the bed, preparing breakfast, washing a car, taking out the garbage, walking the dog, etc.

Now write two versions of a monologue in which the character explains the steps that he/she takes in the activity from start to finish.

Monologue A: Something really good has just happened to your character and they are in an extremely happy mood.

Write Monologue A from your character's point of view having them describe their selected activity. The happy mood that they are in should affect the words they use to recount the activity and how they choose to describe it.

Monologue B: Your character has just received some terrible news.

Now write Monologue B from your character's point of view having them describe the same activity, but this time while they are in a completely different mood. How does the language in the monologue change now that your character is in a sad mood?

In neither monologue should the character reveal why they are in a good or bad mood. Let the mood be present and let it color both monologues so that the language of each version is affected.

16   Additional Dialogue Activities

This session has a number of activities, which can be employed to further develop students' dialogue writing skills. The activities can be used independent of one another or as warm-ups or do-nows. In addition to the activities, I've also listed a few pieces of advice to keep in mind and share with your students as they are writing.

Activity: Analyzing Dialogue Work

In the addendum section, there is an excerpt of a play by Casey Corrado called *The Ivy League* (worksheet I). Casey wrote *The Ivy League* when she was in 8th grade and like Micah Greenleaf's play, her script was selected as part of the Eugene O'Neill Theater Center's Young Playwrights Festival. Make copies of the excerpt, complete with accompanying directions, and hand them out. Have students work in pairs to read the dialogue out loud and then to answer the follow-up questions analyzing Casey's dialogue work.

There is a question on the worksheet that asks students what they think the play might be about and who the main character is. After they've completed the worksheet, share with them Casey's blurb from her empowering spy caper comedy:

> *Ivy is back in her hometown. Everything is fine until she meets up with Conner, an old friend, and Sarah, his new girlfriend. Now she has to convince Conner of Sarah's wrongdoings, tell him the secrets she has been hiding for eleven years, and save the Boston Museum of Fine Arts. All in one night!*

Even how we order a cup of coffee can be a character clue, as Casey shows us with Sarah's dialogue. If you have access to the internet in your classroom, consider showing students the short clip from *When Harry Met Sally* where Sally orders pie. In thirty-five seconds, Nora Ephron (the screenwriter) clearly establishes individual character through the difference in how Harry and Sally order their food.

Activity: What's in a Word?

Generally speaking, we have become somewhat loose with language. Whereas a word like "awesome" used to refer to something that specifically inspired awe, now it is often used interchangeably with words like "cool" or "amazing" or "fantastic". As playwrights, we have the option to be very specific with language or play it a bit loose. As far as I'm concerned, it all depends on the character who we are writing for.

Write the phrase, "S/he _____ into the room" on the board. Then ask for a volunteer. Without letting the class overhear you, tell the volunteer to step outside of the classroom, then simply walk in to the room. After this has been done, ask the class what verb the volunteer exhibited. Most likely, they will say, "she walked into the room". Now again without students hearing, ask the volunteer to "stroll" into the room. How has her gait altered? Were students able to guess the verb?

Ask for other volunteers and repeat with different active verbs.

Examples: walked, stumbled, slithered, skunked, hopped, ambled, wandered, barreled, glided, harrumphed, dawdled, strutted, trudged, stomped, strolled, plodded, stomped, tiptoed, floated, marched, traipsed, moseyed, sauntered

Although the sentence, "she walked into the room" would most definitely get the job done, as writers we can add hints of character by our word choices, so choose the words that most adequately convey the language of your character.

Activity: Overheard Dialogue

Strong dialogue, is most often, natural sounding. A good way of getting the hang of writing natural sounding dialogue is to pay closer attention to how people actually speak.

Tell students that for homework, they are to listen to a conversation between two people and then do their best to write it down verbatim including every pause and "um" and "like" and any other habits the speakers might have.

Good places for aural study: the bus, the playground, the lunchroom, a coffee shop, the park. If students are unable to get to one of these places easily, have them listen to somebody talking on the phone and then write down the actual dialogue they hear as well as the imagined dialogue on the other end.

Have students share their observation conversations with a partner. What are things they discovered about dialogue and character?

The more we observe, the more we take in. And the more we take in, the better attuned we are to how people actually speak.

Activity: Do-Now Dialogues

In addition to being keen observers of how people speak, another useful exercise is to have students practice the art of dialogue writing of various scenarios, not just of their play idea. Below are some suggested scene starter scenarios and opening lines to get their creative juices flowing. Choose one as a prompt for a warm-up or a do-now, but feel free to repeat the activity multiple times with a different prompt. As with all scene writing work, emphasize the need for character-specific language and a clear beginning, middle and end to the scene. Recommend a two-page limit on these dialogues.

Scene Starters
- A surfer being interviewed by a coffee shop manager for a job.
- A teacher and a parent discussing the bad grades of the parent's kid.
- A city kid trying to show her country cousin the ropes.
- A shoe salesperson determined to make a sale.
- Two young kids in a park both wanting to get on the same swing.
- A cheerleader, running for school class president, accuses her friend of not supporting her.
- A girl who wants to break up with her boyfriend for being too needy.
- A boy who wants to break up with his girlfriend because she's too nice.

Opening Lines
- Your father's not going to be happy when he learns of this, Tae.
- I'm sorry, miss, but I ordered an omelet with extra cheese.
- Ma'am, I'm going to have to ask you to put your laptop away now.
- I don't think he understands me, Marge, how do you say bread in French?
- Ms. Aberdeen, I'm afraid your account has been suspended.
- Three more rounds of squats and sit-ups and then you're almost done.
- I believe that all objects have a spiritual side to them. Take this chair, for example.
- I say, old chap, it's a shame that your horse hasn't qualified for the derby.

Activity: Show Don't Tell

Students are often accustomed to narrators telling a story, but in plays, it's much better to have action tell the story as opposed to a person telling us what is happening. The tried and true edict of *show, don't tell* reigns supreme, especially when it comes to the obvious.

Consider this: a character comes on stage and says, "I'm scared" versus a character suddenly cowering behind a chair. The phrase "I'm scared" is made redundant by the action of hiding. This is not to say that everything should be demonstrated or mimed, but if there is something that doesn't need to be said, find a way to show it or find a way for it to come about circuitously.

Option A: Have students write a scene where two characters are scared or angry or in love, but never say so directly. Instead the overriding emotion must be made clear by how they act and interact with one another.

Option B: Have students write a short scene between two people with the first line being: "I told you not to bring it." Nowhere in the scene should they explicitly say what "it" is, but by the scene's end, it should be clear to the audience.

17 Performance Crash Course

Introduce: The Topic of Performing

Many, many a moon ago, before television and the internet, before even telephones and toasters, plays, in addition to being performed, were often read. By flickering candlelight. By the light of the silvery moon.

But that is not really the case any longer. Plays are meant to be heard and they are meant to be performed. So unless you have a readily available cast of actors available, your students will be the performers of these plays.

And in order to get them to ready for the stage, it's time for a quick and easy performance crash course.

Do Now: Signs of a Good Actor

With your students, brainstorm a list of "Signs of a Good Actor" on the board. The more suggestions the better. They will no doubt get phrases like "be loud" or "speak clearly". When the list is complete, either add or circle the following three traits:

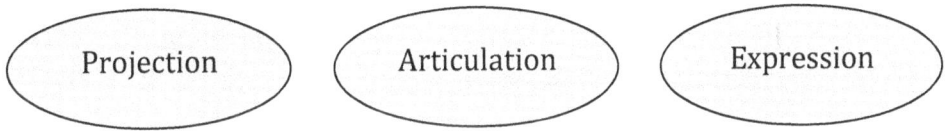

Ask for volunteers to review the definitions of these three points and why they are so important to an actor.

Vocabulary   **Projection – The ability to speak with volume and clarity.**

Articulation – The act of speaking thoughts and concepts clearly.

Expression – The act of conveying one's emotions with believability.

Warm-Up: Vocal Warm-Up

Ask students what are ways that a basketball player warms up before the big game. How about a ballerina? Now how about an actor? What muscles do actors typically use that the other two occupations don't?

Since actors have to speak and be heard (sometimes from quite a distance) it is important that they warm-up their vocal and facial muscles. First demonstrate each below exercise for the class, then have students follow:

- Stretch the face out as if it were the size of a giant watermelon
- Add a big "ahh" to the watermelon face
- Squish the face as if it were a baby raisin
- Add a nasally "eee" to the raisin face
- Alternate between expansive watermelon and shriveled up raisin
- Return to neutral
- Silently yawn as wide as possible
- Yawn again, but this time with sound
- Yawn on sound starting with a high pitch and ending in a low pitch
- Now yawn on sound starting on a low pitch and ending on a high one
- Stretch out the tongue
- Add sound to the tongue stretch
- Mime chewing the world's largest piece of bubble gum
- Add sound to the chewing action

Activity: Tongue Twisters

Practice
Tongue twisters are a great way to practice articulation and enunciation. I always find that a call and response method works best to begin. Below are three examples. Ask students to repeat each word after you, then repeat each short phrase after you. Practice each phrase together a few times, then ask for volunteers to go it solo. The goal is to be able to say the phrase three times clearly without stumbling. Speed isn't as much of the objective as clarity is.

Examples: Topeka Bodega
Unique New York
Are our eyes our own?

After a few, hopefully fun and funny attempts, share a few clues with them: The more they use their mouth muscles and exaggerate (as opposed to mumbling) the phrase, and the more they make sense of what it is they are saying, the easier the tongue twister is to say.

Pop, Bounce, Hiss

Divide the class into small groups. Give them the brief that they have three minutes to write and practice a tongue twister of their own with either the letter P, B or S. Whichever letter they choose:

        P's should **Pop**   **B's** should **bounce**   **S's** should **Hiss**

Examples:
- *Pedro Pear played piano while Papa played piccolo poignantly.*
- *Before Bonnie brought baby baboons, Bonnie bought brownish bananas.*
- *Silly Sandy Sue said she'd sell seventy scented seashells.*

The other choice is to have them write a tongue twister with which to challenge another group. Either method works. The second one requires a bit more time for practice.

Activity: Color Your Words

In order to work on expression, ask students to repeat after you. Whereas you will say the word neutrally, ask them to "color their words" by adding expression when it is their turn. For example, how would they say the word "cold" to show that they were cold? Perhaps shoulders shiver as they stutter on the "c" of "c-c-c-cold". Start with simple concepts, then move on to more complex ones. Do this as a group, but as you progress, start calling on volunteers to share their interpretation or if you see a particularly illuminating example, ask that student to repeat it for everyone else. This is also a good time to fit in any vocabulary words you might be working on in class.

cold	scary	suspicious	rich
freezing	angry	secretive	elderly
warm	excited	quiet	baby-talk
breezy	evil	sad	fabulous
thirsty	small	miserable	bored
giggly	proud	passionate	shocked
relaxed	embarrassed	triumphant	British
honor	unsure	loud	peaceful
guilt	innocent	nervous	agitated
goofy	mysterious	overconfident	calm

Activity: Energy Ball

Now that their voices are warmed up, time to warm-up the imagination. Clear desks and have students join you in standing in a circle. With your hands in front of you about six inches apart from each other, tell students that in your hand you have an energy ball. It looks like this (move imaginary ball in a circle) and sounds like this (accompany moving ball gesture with a sound – an electric zzzzzz works well). You will pass it to the person on your right who will pass it to the person on his right and so forth till it has made its way back to you. The energy ball must maintain the same energy and size that you first endowed it with. Have a practice go. Was the size and sound consistent? Did everybody keep the energy up? Try it again, this time removing any sort of gaps or dead space. Ideally, it should sound like one consistent, electric whorl of energy. And now is when the energy ball starts shifting energy. Tell students that for some reason, the energy ball has now gotten really heavy. Mime the weight of the ball and transform it into something that feels like a two-ton weight. Again pass it to your right and send it onwards around the circle. How exaggerated, yet believable, can students be? This is a really fun game that kids seem to love to play. Change the ball's energy a few times. And allow the ball to change with the given energy. For example, when it's "sticky", perhaps it is so sticky that you get it stuck all over your body and you have to remove it with great force and it gets stuck on your neighbor's head. Really have fun with this and encourage them to, as well. After a few goes, feel free to elicit some suggestions from the group.

Examples:
- heavy ball
- sticky ball
- light-as-a-feather ball
- prickly ball
- hot-like-coals ball
- slippery ball
- electric ball
- pulsating ball

Activity: Pair Articulation

Ask for two volunteers to stand about two feet apart from one another while the rest of the class watches from the sides. Student A speaks a line you give them. Student B then speaks the corresponding line you provide. Their job is to enunciate the words and articulate the meaning so that the two sentences are very distinct from one another. Then they both take a step back and repeat the exercise. Each time they step back, they should get louder so that their partner can clearly hear them. If a line is not projected, articulated or enunciated, anybody can raise their hand and the pair has to repeat that step again. Once the volunteers are done, have the class divide in two and line up opposite each other. Repeat the exercise with everybody working at once. Students should block out the rest of the classroom noise and only focus on communicating with their partner. Encourage them to not use gestures or mime to emphasize their meaning, but use only the words given.

A: That's an ice sculpture.
A: Summer school's breeze.
A: What a good president.
A: Look at a near ring.
A: The dog's not there.
A: I axed the obvious.
A: Five more minutes to eight.
A: That ship, grandma.
A: Go get some ice.
A: Know the snow's wet.
A: Some dwell elsewhere.
A: I see your two eyes.

B: That's a nice sculpture.
B: Summer's cool breeze.
B: What a good precedent.
B: Look at an earring.
B: The dog snot there.
B: I asked the obvious.
B: Five more minutes to wait.
B: That's hip, grandma.
B: Go get some mice.
B: No, the snow sweat.
B: Summed well elsewhere.
B: I see you are too wise.

Activity: Emotional Remote Control

Ask for a bold volunteer.

Tell students you have a remote control that controls the volunteer's emotions. The control has a dial that goes from 1 to 10. 1 is low energy and not a lot of volume or emotion and 10 is giving it everything with full-on energy, emotion and volume. 5 is obviously the halfway point, but worth reviewing. Give the volunteer a single sentence.

> **Example**: *You can't handle the truth.*

She will only speak this one sentence, but will do so ten times from level 1 to 10 while you mark off the dial numbers beginning with number one. Advise the volunteer to pace herself and not start off too strong or she won't have enough power left to get to the higher numbers. Keep the audience engaged by asking them questions. If students are having fun with it, feel free to keep going. You could try a paired example and have them go 1 to 10 in the same direction or have one go 1 to 10 and the other go 10 to 1. You could also have all students pair up and do this at the same time with their partner.

> **Example**: A: *You said you wouldn't leave.*
> B: *You said you were going to change.*

Remind everybody that it's not about screeching at 10, but rather their emotions and intensity being a 10 – which is very different.

Activity: Subtext Channel Changer

Review the difference between text and subtext. Ask students if they always say what they mean. Can they think of an example when somebody says one thing, but means another?

Ask for another volunteer and give them a short piece of text. Tell them that they must speak the text, but change the subtext of the sentence when you flip the subtext switch. Have them say the phrase in neutral at first, then try other interpretations.

> **Text**: *She's so nice.*
>
> **Subtext**: I think I can trick her into giving me all her money.
> Nice people bore me.
> Mom will never like me as much as her.
> I sincerely feel sorry for her.
>
> **Text**: *Please, pass the peas.*
>
> **Subtext**: Don't make this harder than it already is.
> I'm really sorry that your grandfather died.
> Why can't you ever pay attention to me?
> I can't believe you're late again.
> I love you more than you will ever know.

Remind students that we don't always say what we mean. And sometimes, we don't always mean what we say. The same can be true for a character in a play. A character's subtext, however, should not go against the playwright's intention.

Activity: Greetings by Number

Have everybody pair up, with one partner as A and the other as B. Have all the A's get in one line and all the B's get in another line. There should be two long lines with the paired A's and B's directly opposite one another. Give each group their line of dialogue and tell them that it is the only text that they can speak.

> Line A's dialogue: *1 – 2 – 3 – 4 – 5*
> Line B's dialogue: *6 – 7 – 8 – 9 – 10*

A's should think of their dialogue as meaning "Hi. How are you?" And B's should think of their dialogue as "I'm doing fine. Thanks for asking." But in reality, they can only say "*1 – 2 – 3 – 4 – 5*" and "*6 – 7 – 8 – 9 – 10*".

When you say "Go", they should approach their partner. A then says his line and B answers with her line. After the exchange they should cross each other as if continuing on their merry way. B should now be standing in A's original position. And vice versa.

Try the dialogue exchange once neutrally. Then tell them to greet each other as if they were:

complete strangers	robots	hiding a secret
long lost friends	spies	parent / child
listening to music	dancers	absentminded
late for a meeting	soldiers	under water
from outer space	rock stars	elderly people
covering up emotions	cowboys	preoccupied

Activity: Performing a Poem

Pick a short poem that can easily be divided up into different sections. I like to use *Come to the Edge* by Christopher Logue because it's a poem that has distinguishable segments; it tells a story succinctly and effectively; and it also offers clear imagery and a message worth exploring with students.

> Come to the edge.
> We might fall.
> Come to the edge.
> It's too high!
> COME TO THE EDGE!
> And they came,
> and he pushed,
> and they flew.

By Christopher Logue
Copyright © Christopher Logue, 1969.

Read the poem out loud to your group, then write it out on the board. Be sure to include the poem's punctuation and capitalization. Ask students what they think the poem is about? What's its message? If they were to perform this as a group, how could it be divided up for more than one speaker? How many different voices does the piece seem to incorporate?

The poem can be divided into three distinct parts: A is an active voice
                                                      B is a passive voice
                                                      C is an outside voice

Divide the class into three groups (A, B, C). And have them practice their group's lines after they've already sussed out which line goes with which group:

Line 1	A	Line 5	A
Line 2	B	Line 6	C
Line 3	A	Line 7	C
Line 4	B	Line 8	C

What is the mood of each group's collective character? How is C's character different than the other two? Does their group's character go through a change? How can they vocally express the change? How is punctuation used to help the reader and the actor understand Logue's intentions?

It's the actor's job to convey the author's intent. In the case of Logue's poem: the A's get more emphatic as they repeat their one line – especially when it is all in capital letters followed by an exclamation point; the B's get more insistent with their fear; while the C's are the measured narrators of the group.

As you've already done the *Emotional Remote Control* activity, have groups decide on what emotional level their lines should be spoken. (My recommendation is to never go below 4 or 5. Even a stage whisper can be performed at a 6.) Feel free to tweak and even conduct their volume and energy. Practice groups separately, while the others act as audience and responders. Can the A's – without screaming – start off at emotional volume

6, then move to 7, then to 9? Can B's jump straight from 7 to 10? Can C's consistently, convincingly and in unison stay at level 8? What happens if some simple movement or gesture is added to illuminate the text?

Play around as much as you like with delivery and pace, and remind students to perform the poem using projection, articulation and expression.

Reflection: All the attention that students gave to Logue's text is the sort of attention they should give to their classmates' words. Actors are such an integral part to a play; they have the power to make things come alive. In order to do that, they must warm-up, rehearse and prepare. And never forget to project, articulate, and express themselves.

Follow-Up: If parts and scripts are already assigned and there are enough copies to go around, send scripts home with students and have them highlight their part(s) and run through their lines a few times.

General Performing Advice

- Do not fidget when it is not your turn to speak or even if it is your turn.

- Hold the script so that it does not block your face. Audiences want to be able to both hear and see you.

- Speak the words written by the playwright. This means do not, under any circumstance, improvise dialogue for the role you are playing.

- Instead of always keeping your eyes on the script, see if you can look and interact with the other students who are acting.

- Likewise, be sure to lift your face from the script so that the audience can connect with you, as well.

- Speak clearly, deliberately and with volume.

- If the audience laughs at a joke, wait for the laughter to die down a bit so that they don't miss the next line of dialogue.

- If you notice that a mistake has been made by you or another actor, don't let the audience know it was a mistake. Keep going.

- And, of course, have fun!

Opportunities for Young Playwrights

Below are a few competitions and festivals for young playwrights that are either national or regional. These are all in operation at the time of publication*, but to find out further details and competition requirements, go to the organization's website. If playwrights have follow-up questions, they can always email the contact person, but I recommend that they read up on the organizations first and foremost. For local or state-specific opportunities, check with local theater companies, arts organizations or do an online search.

Blank Theatre Company's Young Playwrights Festival
Location: California
Eligibility: ages 9-19
Website: www.theblank.com

Eugene O'Neill Theater Center's Young Playwrights Festival
Location: Connecticut
Eligibility: ages 12-18 and must be in middle or high school
Website: www.theoneill.org/professional-development-and-education/ypf

Kennedy Center's VSA Playwright Discovery Award Program
Location: Washington DC
Eligibility: grades 6-12
Website: www.kennedy-center.org/education/vsa/programs/playwright_discovery.cfm

Scholastic Arts and Writing Award
Location: New York
Eligibility: grades 7-12
Website: www.artandwriting.org

Young Playwrights Inc.'s National Playwriting Competition
Location: New York
Eligibility: ages 18 and under
Website: www.youngplaywrights.org
* Currently, YPI is restructuring; please check their website for updates.

Youth Play's New Voices One-Act Competition
Location: California
Eligibility: ages 19 and under
Website: www.youthplays.com/submit_play.php

Vocabulary

Antagonist — The person opposing the protagonist.

Articulation — The act of speaking thoughts and concepts clearly.

Audience — The group of people who watch the play.

Axial — Movement in a fixed place.

Character — A person portrayed in a play (who the actor pretends to be).

Climax — The turning point or high point of the story.

Complications — See *rising action*.

Conflict — The dramatic struggle between two forces or a problem that must be solved.

Denouement — The conclusion or resolution of the play (French for "unraveling").

Dialogue — A conversation between two people or more.

Exposition — The beginning part of a play that gives important background information on character and situation.

Expression — The act of conveying one's emotions with believability.

Falling Action — The series of events that happen after the climax.

Genre — The type or kind of play style (comedy, tragedy, melodrama, tragicomedy).

Improvisation — The act of creating and performing something spontaneously and without preparation.

Inciting Incident — The event that jumpstarts the action of the play (after the exposition).

Locomotive — Movement through space.

Monologue — A long and uninterrupted speech made by one actor.

Obstacles	Something that gets in the way of what a character wants.
Play	A literary piece meant to be performed live by actors (usually on a stage).
Playwright	The person who writes the play. (Notice that the noun is spelled with "wright" as opposed to "write". Originally, a "wright" was known as a builder or creator of something. And so a playwright is a builder and creator of plays.)
Plot	The organized pattern of events that make up a play.
Projection	The ability to speak with volume and clarity.
Prop	A portable object that is used on the set of a play (short for properties).
Protagonist	The central character of a play (and, typically, who the audiences relates to most.)
Rising Action	A series of events following the inciting incident that develops conflict and/or character and leads up to the climax of the play; also referred to as *complications.*
Scene	The subdivision of an act of a play.
Script	The text of a play (including dialogue and stage directions).
Setting	The time and place where the play happens.
Stage Direction	An instruction in the text of the play.
Subtext	The thoughts and motives beneath the dialogue; what a character really thinks and believes.
Tableau	A frozen picture representing a moment in time (plural: tableaux).
Theme	The basic idea or subject of a play.

20 Worksheet Index

The nine worksheets are sometimes used more than once throughout the book. For quick reference, see listed pages below.

A. Comparing Different Types of Text .... page 6

B. Play Excerpt I - *The Foxwoods Dilemma* .... pages 9, 19

C. Plot Diagram .... pages 21, 23, 47

D. The Eight W's of Character Development .... pages 29, 35, 39, 41, 47, 52, 63

E. House A .... pages 29, 42

F. House B .... pages 29, 42

G. Play Framework .... pages 48, 49, 53, 61

H. Script Formatting .... pages 50, 56

I. Play Excerpt II - *The Ivy League* .... page 78

Worksheet A: Comparing Different Types of Text

Text 1

Ali, a shy, but proud girl, is sitting by herself in a busy café pretending to read a book. She has a cup of tea and a half eaten tuna sandwich in front of her. Every once in awhile she looks at the empty seat next to her and quietly mumbles something towards it. Just as she is about to randomly turn the page of her book, Jay walks by. "Is this seat taken?" he asks. Ali doesn't want to be rude, but she can't allow Jay to sit there because as far as she's concerned, the seat may look empty, but it is actually taken... by her guardian angel.

Text 2

A girl in a café
Pretends to read a book
All the while mumbling
But no one gives a look

A boy who's bought his lunch
Spies an empty chair
And asks the girl who's reading,
"Mind if I sit there?"

The girl cannot allow
The boy to sit and eat
'Cause her invisible guardian angel
Is sitting in that seat

Text 3

In a busy café.

JAY: Excuse me. Is this seat taken?
ALI: Um... well... *(She closes the book.)* It kind of is.
JAY: Oh, well, do you mind if I sit here till your friend arrives?
ALI: What makes you think I'm waiting for somebody?
JAY: Um. Okay. *(He goes to pull the seat back.)* I'm just going to sit –
ALI: No, don't!
JAY: Why not?
ALI: Just – just please don't.
JAY: Why?
ALI: It's – it's going to sound stupid.
JAY: Lady, there's nowhere else to sit.
ALI: *(Pausing slightly before speaking.)* My guardian angel is sitting there.
JAY: *(Smiling.)* Your guardian angel.
ALI: I knew you wouldn't believe me.
JAY: Look if you didn't want me to sit there, you could have just said so.
ALI: I *don't* want you to sit there!

Worksheet B: Play Excerpt I – *The Foxwoods Dilemma* by Micah Greenleaf

SCENE ONE

(FOXWOODS walks briskly into the room and walks over to his colleague)

FOXWOODS

Francis! How could you consider doing it? How could this benefit anyone?

FRANCIS

Now, now, Foxwoods, don't jump to conclusions.

FOXWOODS

Jump to conclusions? You are planning to endanger the last patron of the *iguanosa nueve* for an experiment that is destined to fail. You *need* to think this through, recalculate.

FRANCIS

Says the man who plans on genetically replicating the iguana to save the species. How touching. We all look forward to the day the great Professor Foxwoods creates the first working genetic replicator. Remember your first victim? Little Fluffy, wasn't it?

(Seething FOXWOODS glares at his colleague)

FOXWOODS

That was a m-minor miscalculation, I– I used too much power, it was too much for the poor beast. He wasn't supposed to react like that.

(FRANCIS' voice softens to a calm tone)

FRANCIS

Give up, Isaac, you are not well. You must see logic. Please, I do not enjoy watching my colleagues wither away from failure.

FOXWOODS

No, you don't understand, I…

(The assistant then runs into the room)

ASSISTANT

Mr. Foxwoods. I have found the location of your lizard.

FOXWOODS

Where? This is great news!

ASSISTANT

It is in the hands of a certain Ms. Monique De La Fiette. She lives in Buenos Aires, Argentina.

FOXWOODS

Ah! Magnificent! An old colleague of mine! Did you hear that Francis?

(He looks around, but quickly understands)

FOXWOODS

Blast it! He's gone to collect the iguana! This must be stopped.

(FOXWOODS leaves the stage, leaving the assistant bewildered)

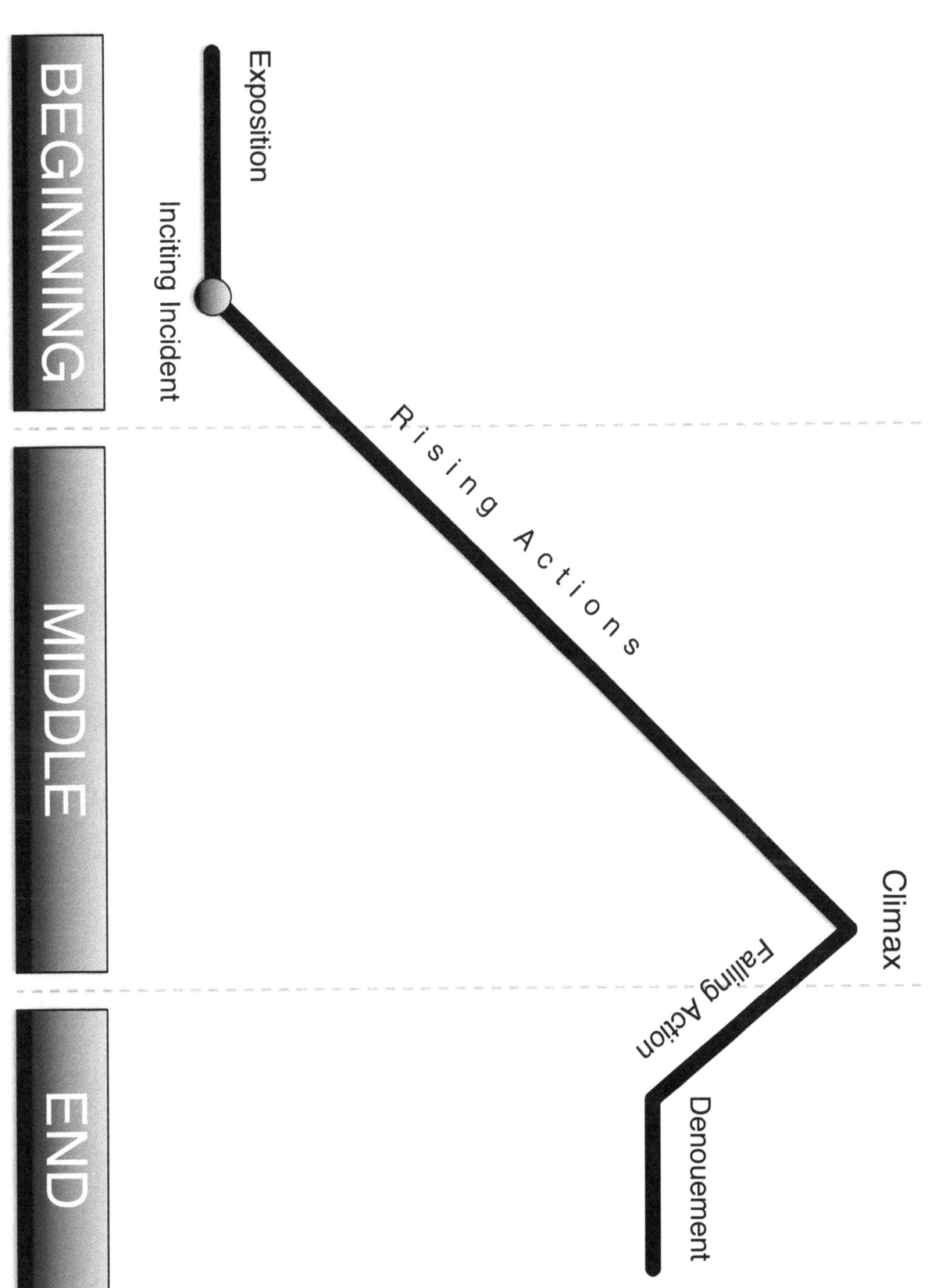

Worksheet D: The Eight W's of Character Development

Student Name: _____

1. **W**ho:

2. **W**hat Age:

3. **W**here:

4. **W**hen:

5. **W**hat does he/she want:

6. **W**hy does he/she want it:

7. **W**hat does he/she do to get it:

8. **W**ho or **W**hat gets in the way:

What are a few words or phrases your character likes to say? And what are other important details to know about your character or their story?

Worksheet E: House A

Worksheet F: House B

Worksheet G: Play Framework

Name _____

Story Sketch

Exposition and Inciting Incident

Main Character's Name:

Main Character's Want:

Main Inciting Incident:

Main Conflict/Problem:

Rising Actions

Complication #1:

Complication #2:

Complication #3:

Climax and Afterwards

Climax Question:

Climax Answer:

Falling Action/Denouement:

Plot Diagram

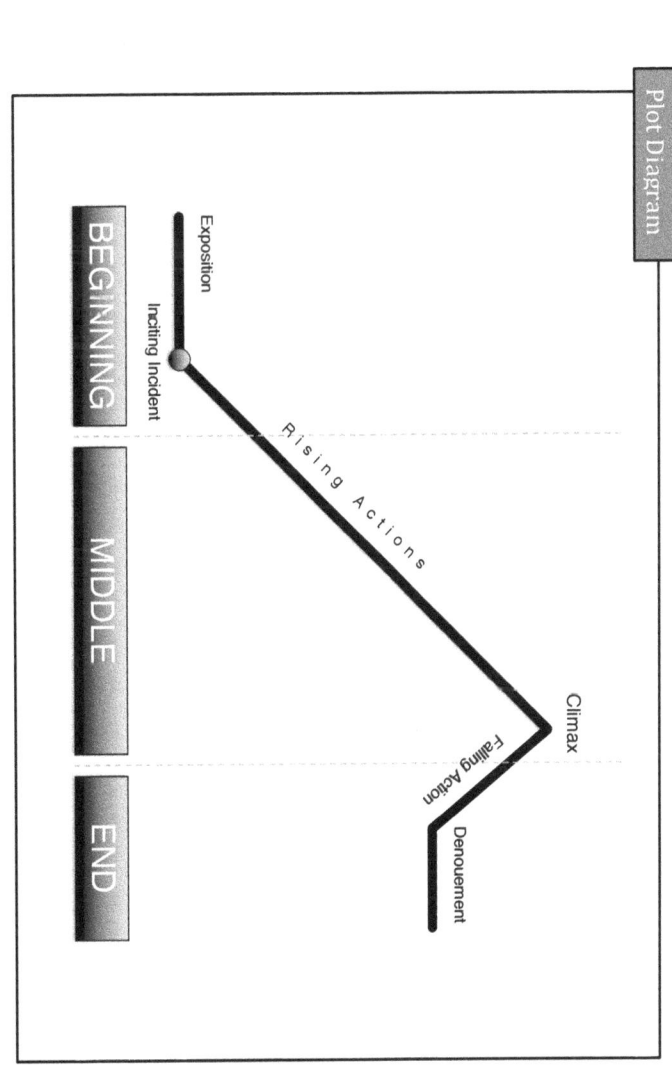

Play Notes

Worksheet H: Script Formatting

If students are submitting their play competitively, have them check the script formatting requirements of that particular competition. A separate title page with contact information as well as a character page will most likely be required.

Professional formatting can vary slightly from script to script. The layout at right allows ample room for note taking, for both playwright and actor, and is ideal for classroom work.

SCENE 1

(*Morning. Inside a classroom. At the onset, have stage directions mention the time and place of the scene. Place stage directions in italics and have them positioned 2 tabs away from the left hand margin.*)

CHARACTER #1

Your Character name should be placed 3 tab stops over from the left hand margin and be in all caps. Do not indent the Dialogue or put it in quotes.

CHARACTER #2

Use a standard Times New Roman or Courier 12-point font.

CHARACTER #1

As for the page margins, go with one inch on the top, bottom and right side of the page and then 1.50 on the left and right.

(*If you have stage directions between lines, place them between the dialogue like so. Also when referring to CHARACTERS in the stage directions, their names should appear in all caps.*)

CHARACTER #2

Did you notice that the Character dialogue is not double spaced within the lines, but there is a double space between the Characters?

CHARACTER #1

(Softly)

If you would like to include a note as to how a line should be delivered, it will go 2 tab stops over from the left hand margin, under the character's name. These delivery notes should be limited to one to two words only and should not be italicized. Use them very sparingly.

CHARACTER #2

Oh, and don't forget to number your pages.

CHARACTER #1

That's all for now. Have fun formatting your script!

End of Scene

Worksheet I: Play Excerpt II – *The Ivy League* by Casey Corrado

Below is an excerpt from the second scene of a play called *The Ivy League* written by Casey Corrado when she was in the 8th grade. Read the exchange out loud with a partner, then together answer the questions on the right.

Conner is working at a coffee shop when Ivy, a girl he went to high school with and hasn't seen in three years, enters. As the two are catching up, suddenly Sarah, Conner's girlfriend, enters the scene...

SARAH

Conner! Who's your friend?

CONNER

Oh, Sarah. This is my friend Ivy from high school. I told you about her, right?

SARAH

So this is the famous Ivy. Conner has told me all about you. *(Turns to CONNER)* Why don't you go get something for us to drink while we chit-chat?

CONNER

Oh, right! Hot chocolate for you and...? What do you want, Sarah?

SARAH

A cappuccino with extra sugar and sprinkle a pinch of ground cinnamon on top.

CONNER

(Takes pad of paper out of his apron) Umm... Okay... *(Writes on the pad of paper)*

SARAH

Oh, and Conner? Don't forget to use fake sugar. You know how I like it.

CONNER

Okay.

SARAH

Thanks, sweetie!

- What kind of person do you think Sarah is based on her dialogue?

- How does her dialogue help inform us about her character?

- What kind of person do you think Conner is based on his dialogue?

- How does his dialogue help inform us about his character?

- What do we learn about Conner and Sarah's relationship from their exchange?

- Even though Ivy doesn't speak in this brief exchange, what do we learn about her?

- Why do you think Sarah refers to her as "the famous Ivy"?

- What do you think Sarah wants to "chit-chat" about with Ivy?

- Who do you think is the main character of the play and why?

- What do you think the play is going to be about?

Acknowledgements

Thanks goes out to all the teachers who have opened their classrooms to me over the years and allowed me to put into practice what I write about in this book. Being in schools has been a very useful – and fertile – training ground. Additional thanks goes to the organizations I have worked with for the past twenty or so years which have allowed me to hone my skills and practice my craft in a stimulating environment. Special thanks to Alison Stahl for being a terrific sounding board and giving collaborator; Ron Lavine for being the most impactful teacher I ever had the pleasure of learning from; Karen Curlee, Stephen DiMenna, and Mark Erson who introduced me to some of the ideas in chapters two and six; to both Micah Greenleaf and Casey Corrado for granting me permission to excerpt from their plays; and to Denver Casado and Linda Trinh for invaluable editing input. On a personal acknowledgement level... thank you to Maggie, Shefket, Sabrina and Sammy. And most of all, thank you to Michael, who not only encouraged me to write this book, but also offered me insightful and thought-provoking feedback all along the way.

About the Author

Sophia Chapadjiev is a writer originally from Chicago now dividing her time between the US and the UK. Sophia teaches playwriting and musical theatre writing and she is also the Artistic Director of the Young Playwrights Festival at the Eugene O'Neill Theater Center where she has been Director of Education since 2007. She has also facilitated professional development workshops at various educational conferences. Selected NYC productions include: *Over the Moon* (Best Play, plus Audience Favorite; American Globe Theater); *Aloha Flight 243* (HERE Arts Center); and *First Odd Prime* (Players Theater). Most recently, her play, *In This House*, was selected for the Dark Horse Festival in London. Sophia has a BFA from Emerson and an MFA from NYU's Graduate Musical Theatre Writing Program.

www.ingramcontent.com/pod-product-compliance
Lightning Source LLC
Chambersburg PA
CBHW080552170426
43195CB00016B/2763